NEW DIRECTIONS
IN
GREEK AMERICAN STUDIES

NEW DIRECTIONS
IN
GREEK AMERICAN STUDIES

Edited by
DAN GEORGAKAS
AND
CHARLES C. MOSKOS

PELLA PUBLISHING COMPANY, INC.
NEW YORK, NY 10018-6401
1991

NEW DIRECTIONS
IN
GREEK AMERICAN STUDIES

Library of Congress Catalog Card Number 91-61005

ISBN 0-918618-47-9

PRINTED IN THE UNITED STATES OF AMERICA
BY
ATHENS PRINTING COMPANY
337 West 36th Street
New York, NY 10018-6401

Contents

Foreword

The essays in this volume were first presented at a conference on "The Greek American Experience" held in May 1989 in Minneapolis, Minnesota. The conference had a twofold objective: one was celebratory; the other, scholarly. We were celebrating the opening to research of the Theodore Saloutos Collection and the publication of the guide to that collection. Theodore Saloutos (1910-1980) was a pioneer in Greek American historiography; his *Greeks in the United States* (1964) remains the classic work in the field. As teacher and historian, he was also a leader in the new studies of American immigration and ethnic history. One of the purposes of the conference, therefore, was to commemorate Theodore Saloutos, the historian and the man. The second purpose of the conference was to assess the state of scholarship in Greek American studies, and set the agenda for future research. We hoped the conference would serve as a catalyst for studies by the coming generation of scholars.

We are gratified that the conference apparently succeeded on both counts. The presence of Mrs. Florence Saloutos and the "Saloutos clan," the heartfelt tributes to Professor Saloutos, and the festive banquet with Greek food, music, and dance gave to the event an appropriate celebratory quality.

The generally high and original quality of the twenty-seven presentations provided the scholarly substance of the conference, while Hellenic passion as well as logic was in evidence in the animated discussions that followed. It is this volume which best testifies to the conference's scholarly merits. The formation of a Greek American Studies Association at the conclusion of the conference further suggests that it may indeed have served as a catalyst.

The May 1989 conference was the culmination of a project

which began in 1982 with the donation by Florence Saloutos of Professor Saloutos's library and papers to the Immigration History Research Center of the University of Minnesota. Shortly thereafter, the establishment of the Theodore Saloutos Memorial Fund for Greek American Studies by Mrs. Saloutos, with the indispensable help of Professor Charles Moskos, made possible the processing of the Saloutos Collection. Several hundred Greek Americans and admirers of Professor Saloutos contributed to the fund.

The Saloutos Fund provided significant support for the conference. Other major funding came from the Minnesota Humanities Commission, in cooperation with the National Endowment for the Humanities and the Minnesota State Legislature, and the College of Liberal Arts of the University of Minnesota. The Greek American community of the Twin Cities also contributed in a variety of ways to the success of the conference. To all of these entities, we are pleased to express our deep gratitude for their invaluable help.

Finally, I wish to express my personal appreciation to Judith Rosenblatt, conference coordinator, for a fine job of administration, and to Charles Moskos and Dan Georgakas, who not only provided the intellectual leadership for the conference, but have extended its influence by seeing this volume into print.

It is our fond hope that those who read these essays will be stimulated to pursue further studies of the Greek American experience. To those who are, I wish to extend an open invitation to make use of the rich resources that await you in the Theodore Saloutos Collection.

RUDOLPH J. VECOLI
Director, Immigration History Research Center
University of Minnesota

Introduction

Greek American studies can be understood as the effort to relate academic research, intellectual understanding, and artistic expression to the manifold and ongoing experience of Americans of Greek ancestry. Although Greek American studies as a formal subject area can hardly be said to exist, the outlines of a cumulative scholarship are becoming discernible for the first time. More has been written on Greek Americans in the 1980s than in all previous years combined.[1]

The emergence of Greek American studies are even more remarkable since almost all who currently write about Greek Americans do so as a secondary interest. Not a single university-based historian studies Greek Americans as a main research subject. This situation can be blamed partially on the small market for Greek American studies, a state of affairs that does not reflect well on an ethnic group that takes enormous pride in its high levels of formal education. But the problem is more than just a matter of demand. With its inevitable focus on immigrant life, Greek American studies are *declasse* among most scholars who deal with contemporary Greece. One of the accomplishments of scholars of modern Greece has been to assert the legitimacy of their subject matter by separating it from Classical Greek and Byzantine studies. In parallel fashion, Greek American studies will remain undeveloped unless separated from modern Greek studies.

A major threshold in Greek American studies was crossed at "The Greek American Experience: A Conference on the State of Scholarship and an Agenda for the Future," sponsored by

---

[1]See the selected bibliography in Charles C. Moskos, *Greek Americans: Struggle and Success* (New Brunswick: Transaction Publishers, 1989). Revised and expanded version of the 1980 work of the same title.

the Immigration History Research Center (IHRC) of the University of Minnesota in May 1989.[2] Our debt is enormous to Rudolph Vecoli, IHRC director, who took the initiative to organize the conference. The major objective of the event was to commemorate the preservation and cataloguing of the papers of Theodore Saloutos (1910-1980), the dean of Greek American historiography.[3] Born in Milwaukee of immigrant working-class

[2]The first major scholarly conference held on Greek American studies was "The Greek Experience in America," sponsored by Symposium '76, the Illinois Bicentennial Commission, and the Modern Greek Studies Association, Chicago, Illinois, October 29-31, 1976. Organizers were Andrew T. Kopan and Alexander Karanikas; program chair was Charles C. Moskos. In scale and scope, this conference was not equaled until the May 11-14, 1989, conference sponsored by the Immigration History Research Center.

Only three other conferences dealing exclusively or primarily with the Greek American experience were held before 1980: the "Greek American Bilingual Bicultural Education Conference," sponsored by the Hellenic American Neighborhood Action Committee, New York City, April 25, 1975; "Psycho-Social Perspectives of the Greek American Community," sponsored by the Hellenic American Neighborhood Action Committee, the Greek American Behavioral Sciences Institute, and the Order of AHEPA, New York City, March 5, 1977; and "Hellenic-American Identity," sponsored by the Hellenic Professional Society of Illinois, Lake Bluff, Illinois, September 28-30, 1979.

In the 1980s, eleven conferences on Greek American themes were held in addition to the IHRC conference: "The Greek-American Community in Transition," sponsored by the Queens College Center for Byzantine and Modern Greek Studies and the Ikaros Greek Club, New York City, May 9-10, 1980; "The Future of Greek Culture in America," sponsored by the Center for European Studies of the Graduate Center for the City University of New York, the Queens College Center for Byzantine and Modern Greek Studies, and the *Journal of the Hellenic Diaspora*, New York City, March 20, 1982; "Diaspora," sponsored by Krikos, New York City, October 13, 1984; "The Greeks in America: A Celebration of Films," sponsored by Greek-American Community Services, fall 1986; "The Greek-American Family: Continuity Through Change," sponsored by the Immigration History Research Center, University of Minnesota, St. Paul, Minnesota, June 9-10, 1984; "Issues and Prospects for the Survival of the Greek-American Community into the 21st Century," sponsored by Krikos Midwest chapter, Chicago, Illinois, March 15, 1986; "Education and Greek Americans," sponsored by the Queens College Center for Byzantine and Modern Greek Studies, New York City, May 15-17, 1986; "Greek-American Arts and Letters," sponsored by Krikos, New York City, October 18, 1986; "In Celebration of Greek Women," sponsored by Krikos, New York City, October 17, 1987; "Conflict Between the Old and New Immigrants in the Assyrian and Greek Communities," sponsored by the Assyrian Universal Alliance Foundation and Greek-American Community Services, Chicago, Illinois, October 31-November 1, 1987; and "Yiorti: A Celebration of Greek Womanhood," sponsored by Greek Heritage Society of Southern California, Los Angeles, California, May 14, 1988.

[3]See Louise Martin, compiler, *Guide to the Theodore Saloutos Collection* (St. Paul, MN: Immigration History Research Center, University of Minnesota,

parents, Saloutos became a professor of history at the University of California at Los Angeles. Before he began to work in Greek American history, he established a national reputation as a historian of American agriculture. In 1964, Saloutos published his monumental work in the field of Greek American studies, *The Greeks in the United States.*[4] Subsequently, he continued to write extensively about Greek Americans, including the posthumously published entry on Greek Americans in the *Harvard Encyclopedia of American Ethnic Groups.* Saloutos was not enthralled either with oral history or with cliometricians' numbers. He was an old-fashioned narrative historian who relied mainly on the printed word for sources. His papers have been preserved and catalogued at the Immigration History Research Center. No other collection of Greek Americana approaches the range of the Saloutos Archives.

At the conclusion of the University of Minnesota conference, a Committee for Greek American Studies was established.[5] Among the Committee's goals was to seek publication of the twenty-seven papers presented at the conference, to work toward creating a definitive Greek American bibliography, and to establish a newsletter for ongoing communications.[6] The publishing goals of the Committee are partly being met by this volume, which represents a selection of those papers that in our judgment opened up new or neglected research areas in Greek American studies. Some of the contributors have academic positions, others are independent scholars, but all are exceptionally qualified to advance our understanding of the Greek experience in America.

The first three essays deal in whole or in part with the nineteenth century, a period when the Greeks in America numbered only in the thousands. Eva Catafygiotu Topping examines the

1988). Charles C. Moskos and Florence Saloutos were the co-chairs of the Theodore Saloutos Memorial Fund drive that made this project possible.

[4]Now out of print. (Cambridge: Harvard University Press, 1964.)

[5]The following officers were elected at the establishment of the Committee for Greek American Studies on May 13, 1989, in the kitchen of the IHRC: Peter N. Marudas, chairperson; first vice chair: George D. Tselos; second vice chair: Vasilikie Demos; recording secretary: Steven Frangos; and newsletter editor: Dan Georgakas.

[6]Greek-American Studies Newsletter, Queens College, Byzantine and Modern Greek Studies Program, 65-30 Kissena Boulevard, Flushing, NY 11367-0904. Provides a continuing update on these and other projects.

life of one of the two-score young Greeks who came to the United States as refugees from the upheavals and dangers associated with the Greek Revolution of 1821. Peter W. Dickson contributes a landmark essay on the impact of a single individual and a small area of the Peloponnesus upon the subsequent shape of Greek American communities in the United States. Overlapping in some aspects with Dickson's account, Helen Geracimos Chapin presents a mini-history of the Greeks in Hawaii from the time of their arrival in the late eighteenth century through the modern period.

Our second group of four essays deals with 1900-1945, the period of most intense immigration and the harshest ethnic struggle. Building upon the pioneering work of Helen Zeese Papanikolas and drawing on newly discovered primary sources, Gunther W. Peck offers new insights into the attitudes of Greek miners in Utah. Also working on a labor theme, Dan Georgakas uses the life of Demosthenes Nicas to explore the still largely untold story of the Greek left and to establish new data on the general experience of Greeks who entered the industrial working class, a rarely-discussed segment of the community. Ole L. Smith takes up the theme of Greek music in the United States and discovers that the Greeks in America had a creative as well as preserving role. Alexandros K. Kyrou concludes the section with a detailed account of how the Greeks in America organized a war relief campaign that brought some 750,000 tons of food, medicine, clothing, and supplies into the occupied Greece of the 1940s.

Problems in Greek American studies that have become increasingly evident as the broad outlines of the field have been established are the focus of our final section. Yiorgos Kalogeras evaluates various criteria that need to be considered if one attempts to identify a body of writing as Greek American literature. G. James Patterson discusses a new kind of ethnic identity taking shape in various ethnic communities in the United States. Finally, Constance Callinicos concludes the volume by bringing a feminist analysis to Greek American concerns. Although her immediate topic is arranged marriages, the implications of her analysis touch every aspect of community life.

We do not believe that the essays in this volume necessarily constitute the final word on the subjects addressed. Many, in fact, are early explorations or are intended to be provocative. As a group, they fit into a body of work that is accelerating in quantity and quality. We direct readers to other important papers given at the Saloutos conference which are now available in the *Journal of the Hellenic Diaspora* (Vol. XV, Nos. 1-4) and to the continuing work of various specialists.[7]

Even as a point of crystallization nears for Greek American studies, significant gaps in research remain, especially regarding some institutions that have had a lasting and significant effect on Greek America. The emergence of a reflective scholarship within Greek Orthodoxy in America is promising.[8] Even so, little of this scholarship, clerical or lay, has yet to incorporate the intellectual contributions of the sociology of religion, or to show much of a theoretical or comparative perspective. A full examination of the current welter of trends within the Church—laity assertion, Americanization, pan-Orthodoxy, pristine Orthodoxy, monasticism, feminism, generational change, among others—remains to be performed.

Equally serious gaps also exist with regard to mainstream secular organizations as well. The American Hellenic Educational Progressive Association (AHEPA), the largest and most influential national organization of Greek Americans, has yet to find its historian. Nor has the Greek community of New York City, the largest in the country, ever been the subject of a comprehensive study. Although the Greek American press has lent itself to examination by the very nature of the printed media, Greek-language television and radio have been virtually ignored. Hardly anything has been written about Greek American voting patterns. Just as limited is our knowledge of Greek Americans and their position in the American economy as workers, owners, managers. In this regard, the study of Greeks and restaurants should not be considered frivolous.

The intellectual quandary of Greek American studies arises from the two competing paradigms used to interpret the Greek American experience. One views the Greek Americans as part of

[7]Moskos, *Greek Americans*, pp. 187-192, provides a comprehensive listing of the personalities, events, and issues in Greek American studies.

[8]Moskos, *Greek Americans*, 190-191.

a homeland extension, an *homogenia,* a Hellenic diaspora. The other regards Greek Americans as entrants and then participants in American history. Which of these analytic models best explains the history of the Greeks in America? Which should be the model most valued by community leaders when planning ethnic projects? There is no simple answer, for each of the models contains part of the truth.

The paradigm of the diaspora is that one's cultural roots and political sensitivities must be nourished by a responsiveness to contemporary Greek realities, even if at a distance. The underlying presumption is that, whether residing or even born in the United States, Greeks in America share a destiny somehow connected with other people who call themselves Hellenes and live in any number of nations aside from Greece itself. The diaspora perspective raises profound problems of crisscrossing, perhaps conflicting, loyalties toward Greece and the United States, problems normally hushed up in the Greek American community. As an analytical proposition, the diaspora view implies that the Greek immigrant phenomenon in America is better grasped as a major outcome of the political and economic processes in modern Greece rather than as a minor aspect of the American historical experience.

A quite different view is that Greek Americans must be placed in the broad context of the immigration and ethnic experiences of the United States. Whatever the fullness of their traditional heritage and allegiances to the old country, the Greek immigrants who came to the American shore inevitably reordered their lives. Initially, they may have been tentative in adapting to the imperatives of the economic and social structure of the United States, but, with the passage of time, they have come into greater and greater conformity with American cultural norms. Among those born in the United States, it seems clear that one's identity is typically of an American ethnic rather than of a transplanted Greek. What is different among the American-born is that the range of experience is much more diverse than the relatively common and shared experiences of the immigrant generation. Comprehending this diversity is yet another of the challenges Greek American studies must face.

The competing interpretations of the Greek American experience, and the many areas of that experience still barely researched, indicate that Greek American studies must accept debate about their own nature as part of their recognized subject matter. The editors of and contributors to *New Directions in Greek American Studies* offer this volume as a stimulus and contribution to that debate.

— DAN GEORGAKAS
CHARLES C. MOSKOS

George M. Colvocoresses USN:
From Sea to Shining Sea

EVA CATAFYGIOTU TOPPING

*He saw the cities of many peoples
and learned their ways.*

ODYSSEY, 1.3

In August 1823 the American brig *Margarita* dropped anchor at Baltimore.[1] On board were eight or nine Greek boys.[2] One of them was a "silent and grave" child, Georgios Calvocoresses, a not yet seven-year-old from Chios.[3] Like many another transplanted Greek name, his surname underwent change. An "o" displaced the "a" of the first syllable. Remarkably, however, it

[1] The first biographical sketch of Colvocoresses appeared a century ago in *Appleton's Cyclopaedia of American Biography* I (New York, 1887), pp. 699f. That in the *Dictionary of American Biography* II, Pt. 2 (New York, 1929-1930), pp. 326f., gives the same few basic facts. The article by a grandson gives additional information: Major Harold Colvocoresses, United States Marine Corps, Retired, "Captain George Musalas Colvocoresses, U.S.N.," *The Washington Historical Quarterly* 25 (1934), pp. 163-170.

I wish to express my thanks to Colonel A. P. Colvocoresses and Harold Colvocoresses, great-grandson and great-great-grandson respectively of the Greek immigrant, who graciously answered questions and provided various materials. They made available to me two important, unpublished family documents on which the present essay is principally based: *A Personal Narrative Written for My Family* (hereafter cited as *Narrative*), written in 1861-62 by George M. Colvocoresses and *Records of the Colvocoresses (Colvocoressi) Family* (hereafter cited as *Records*), written in 1896 by his son, Admiral George Partridge Colvocoresses. As he obtained more information about the family, the admiral added notes in the margins.

The date of GMC's arrival is securely established by a letter (March 5, 1824), *Records*, p. 169f.

[2] See Chrestos D. Lazou, *E Amerike kai o rolos tes sten epananastase tou 1821* (America and Her Role in the Revolution of 1821), II (Athens, 1984), p. 562.

[3] *Records*, p. 172, from a letter (March 11, 1824).

escaped abbreviation. All five syllables have survived. To this day, his descendants proudly bear the pentasyllabic Greek name Colvocoresses. The American variant, moreover, has migrated to Chios in the name of a street.

Colvocoresses's fateful voyage westward from Smyrna took fifty days.[4] It was his first long voyage but not the last. During his career as an officer in the United States Navy from 1832 to 1867, Captain George Musalas Colvocoresses criss-crossed the earth's seas, north, south, east and west. Colvocoresses Bay in Antarctica, Colvocoresses Island in the Fijis, Colvos Rocks and Colvos Passage on the coast of Washington document the presence of a Greek in the magnificent voyage that lasted 1,392 days, logging 87,780 miles and proclaiming everywhere the "Manifest Destiny" of the United States.

Continuing the tradition of his great-grandfather, Colonel Alden Partridge Colvocoresses USA recently added to the map Colvocoresses Reef in the Indian Ocean and Colvos Island in the Potomac River, both discovered by and named for him. I believe that the Colvocoresses toponyms are unique in the United States, being the only place names of Greek American origin.

The *Margarita* heads the long list of ships on which Colvocoresses sailed. An American navy man for 35 years, he served on the USS *United States, John Adams, Delaware, Potomac, Alleghany, Germantown, Peacock, Vincennes, Flying Fish, Oregon, Porpoise, Ohio, Warren, Shark, Relief, Levant, Supply, Saratoga, Tuscarora, Dacotah, Wachusett* and *St Marys*. No Greek Odysseus before him had ever sailed in so many ships to so many places.

Colvocoresses belongs to a small distinctive group of Greek immigrants. Between 1823 and 1828 about forty young Greeks, most of them small children, arrived in the United States.[5] Their ages varied from six to twenty-three. Males by far outnumbered females, Sappho, and Garouphalia and her two sisters,

---

[4]*Narrative*, p. 37.

[5]This interesting group has not yet been properly studied. They are usually treated in a page or two in histories of Greeks in America, in which factual errors are often perpetuated. Lazou, *E Amerike* II, pp. 543-668, presents the most extensive treatment yet, but must be used with caution. See also G. A. Kourvetaris, "Greek-American Professionals: 1820's-1970's," *Balkan Studies* 18 (1977), pp. 311f., Appendix I.

being the only girls known of this group. They originated in all parts of the Greek world, in the Aegean and Ionian islands, in Asia Minor and in various provinces of the mainland. Contrary to the general impression, they were not all orphans brought here by philhellenes or the American Foreign Mission Board. For example, Colvocoresses and John Zachos[6] were sent to the New World by their parents. All, however, were refugees from the terrors and upheavals caused by the Greek Revolution of 1821.

Their circumstances and experiences differ dramatically from those of the immigrants who began to arrive later toward the end of the same century. Church organizations and generous philhellenes welcomed these early immigrants and facilitated their entry into American ways and life. The language barrier quickly disappeared. The absence of family, church, and community promoted the process of acculturation and assimilation.

As a result, most of this group, contrary to the original intent, remained in the United States. Several returned to Greece for a while, but then opted for life in their second motherland. The American education and experience of the few who remained in Greece proved valuable. Chrestos Evangelides, the inspiration of William Cullen Bryant's popular poem, "The Greek Boy" (1828), became a successful entrepreneur in Greece and famous as the "Greek Yankee."

Education had prompted the immigration of these Greeks to the United States. They were at once enrolled in the best schools and colleges of that time. In the late 1820s, Mount Pleasant Classical Institute in Amherst, Massachusetts, had not only students from Greece but also several Greek-born instructors. Graduates of Yale, Columbia, Amherst and Kenyon, these first-generation Greek Americans became lawyers, ministers, diplomats, journalists, politicians, naval officers, writers and educators. The variety and number of the books they wrote are impressive: dictionaries, travel books, text books, grammars, political tracts and autobiographies. Byzantinists still use the dictionary published in 1870 by the legendary Harvard professor, Evangelos Apostolides Sophocles (1805-1883), who arrived in

---

[6]See E. C. Topping, "John Zachos: Cincinnatian from Constantinople," *The Cincinnati Historical Society Bulletin* 34 (1976), pp. 47-69; "Greek Zachos: American Educator," *Greek Orthodox Theological Review* 21 (1976), pp. 351-366.

the United States in 1828. In the 1850s thousands of American armchair-travelers read Colvocoresses's account of his travels and adventures in distant lands among exotic primitive peoples.

The life and career of George Musalas Colvocoresses illustrates how these first Greek Americans made their way in nineteenth-century America. Unlike later immigrants, they did not start at the bottom of the socio-economic scale. They stepped off the boat and into the American mainstream.

The eldest of the eight children of Constantine and Franka, nee Grimaldi, Colvocoresses was born on the Aegean island of Chios, October 22, 1816. His parents belonged to old prominent families of mixed "Byzantine," Genoese and Greek descent.[7] His father was a prosperous merchant established in Smyrna, while the family resided on the island. His "solicitous" parents sent him to school "before I could even walk."[8] Although his Greek education was cut short, he had learned to read. When George left for America, he carried with him a copy of the Greek New Testament.[9]

The massacres in Chios by the Turks in April 1822 shocked the world and determined the destiny of this island-lad. Colvocoresses never forgot the tragedy experienced by his family.[10] For his children he recorded how he had seen Turkish "fiends" murder an uncle and his aged grandmother and witnessed "the departure into Asia" of his captive mother and sister. He himself was captured by a "repulsive," one-eyed soldier who "called himself my master."

Six months after ransoming George for 2,000 piastres, Constantine Calvocoresses "formed the resolution" to send his eldest son to America. The six-year-old George boarded the *Margarita* the night before it sailed from Smyrna.[11] William Hilberg, the *Margarita's* first mate, befriended the little immigrant and gave him his first English lesson.[12] Once in Baltimore, George lived

[7]*Records*, pp. 5-19, a detailed, proud account of family origins and genealogy.
[8]*Narrative*, p. 2.
[9]*Records*, pp. 176f. GMC's first English letter (September 20, 1824), written from Vermont to a friend in Baltimore.
[10]*Narrative*, pp. 2-34, a vivid, dramatic account of the traumatic experience that changed the course of his life.
[11]Ibid., p. 36.
[12]*Records*, pp. 169f. In a letter, Hilberg describes George as a "youth of Bright Talents."

for six months in the home (118 Market Street) of Hilberg and his mother.

The refugee from Chios arrived in America at the peak of "Grecian Fever." By 1823-24 sympathy and support for the Greek rebels had spread throughout the country, from Monticello and the White House to remote villages on the frontier in the west. "Greek Committees" organized benefits and successfully tilted American public opinion in favor of the Greek revolutionaries. Philhellenic poetry, journalism and oratory flourished.[13]

In Baltimore, newspapers carried stories about the "Greek boy." Local philhellenes, "influential gentlemen who deeply interested themselves in all that concerned my unfortunate country," appointed themselves George's guardians and planned his future.[14] Dressed in his native garb, George attracted much attention at a large ball held in Baltimore to raise funds for the Greek cause. General Robert Goodloe Harper (1765-1825), veteran of the American Revolution and a prominent philhellene, personally obtained from President Monroe an appointment to West Point for George, available whenever he wished it.[15]

In March 1824, Colvocoresses left Baltimore, traveling northward by stagecoach to Norwich, Vermont. En route, he stopped in New York and New Haven, where he was entertained by the local Greek Committees. For the next eight years George lived and attended school in Norwich. This small New England village on the Connecticut River could not have been more different from the Greek island of his birth.

Having read about the "Greek youth" in the *Baltimore American,* Captain Alden Partridge (1785-1854), formerly superintendent of the Military Academy at West Point, and founder of the American Literary, Scientific and Military Academy in Norwich, had offered George a home and education. In his letter of Februarty 18, 1824, Partridge explained to George's patrons in Baltimore that he "had a deep interest in the welfare"

---

[13]See the discussions by S. A. Larrabee, *Hellas Observed* (New York, 1957), pp. 55-92 and E. C. Topping, "Cincinnati Philhellenism in 1824," *The Cincinnati Historical Society Bulletin* 31 (1973), pp. 127-141.

[14]*Narrative,* pp. 38f.

[15]*Records,* pp. 174-176, the text of General Harper's letter (February 29, 1824) to Captain Partridge regarding Monroe's offer. News of the benefit ball in Baltimore reached Greece. See Lazou, *E Amerike,* I (Athens, 1984), pp. 462-464.

of the Greeks, "this interesting and oppressed people." Moreover, since he had "no children except my pupils," George would
"fill the place of one."[16] The stern, flinty New Englander kept
his promise. Almost four decades later, Colvocoresses wrote of
his benefactor, "He was to me *as a Father*."[17] (The underlining
is by Colvocoresses.) Since Captain Partridge was a bachelor
(he did not marry until 1839), George lived with the family of
his brother, Aaron Partridge, while attending the Academy. On
their farm he kept his own steers and cows.[18]

A school of excellent reputation and high academic standards, Partridge's academy attracted students from all parts of
the country. It drew many students from the South, and a few
from abroad. The prospectus of 1825 lists among the student
body of 480 students four foreign cadets: "Canada 2, Cuba 1,
Island Scio, Greece 1."[19]

Memories of Colvocoresses lasted long in Norwich where he
had been an exotic figure with a definite Greek identity. Seventy
years later, a classmate at the Academy remembered him as a
"Hellene, whose birthplace and Homer's were the same rocky
isle. . . ."[20] Village elders told his son, Admiral Colvocoresses,
how the "boys delighted to excite his quick blood and make
fun of his foreign ways and appearance," especially when Captain Partridge "desired him to wear his Greek costume in the
streets of the village." The son believed that such experiences
may have made his father "the silent, self-contained man that he
was."[21] It is, of course, common for immigrants to be seen and
to see themselves as "other" in their adopted country. Alienation
and rejection are part and parcel of the immigrant experience.

Captain Partridge also used to take his Greek ward to
Dartmouth College, a mile across the river. "The professor of
Greek would have him read before the senior class and say that

[16]*Records*, pp. 63-65, the full text of the letter.

[17]*Narrative*, p. 40.

[18]*Records*, pp. 70f. Captain Partridge approves of George's desire "to be independent."

[19]W. A. Ellis, *Norwich University, 1819-1911: Her History, Her Graduates,
Her Roll of Honor* I (Montpelier VT, 1911), p. 7. A valuable source for the
school's early period.

[20]*Records*, p. 27.

[21]Ibid., p. 68.

he wished his pupils knew Greek as that child did."[22]

George's formal schooling ended when he graduated from the Academy in 1831. Thanks to Partridge's philhellenic generosity, he had received a good education at an elite school, solid training in the humanities, physical and military sciences. Captain Pegram USN, an officer on Midshipman Colvocoresses's first cruise, pronounced him "remarkably well-educated."[23]

In 1831 George's future had to be decided. Whether a return to Greece was discussed then is not known. Earlier, however, in a letter to "Master George Colvocoresses," written from Middletown, Connecticut, March 9, 1827, Partridge had suggested that the Greeks would soon gain independence and "perhaps you may be enabled to render them some assistance."[24] Nor is it known why he did not take the appointment to West Point that had been offered by President Monroe. The reason may be the animosity of Captain Partridge against the army, stemming from the court-martial that had forced his resignation in 1818. In any case, it was Partridge who obtained his appointment to the navy. In February 1832, Colvocoresses began his naval career.

The young Greek immigrant had put down substantial roots in Norwich. Naval leaves were spent in the Vermont village of his childhood. He courted Eliza Freelon Halsey, a local girl, and married her on May 17, 1846. She had been reared in Norwich by her uncle and guardian, Commander Thomas Freelon USN and was an eighth-generation American. Greek-born Lieutenant Colvocoresses had married into a family descended from Manhattan Dutch settlers and pilgrims of Plymouth.

At the time of his marriage, Colvocoresses was "a fine looking young man ... with the straight features of the Greek race." The nineteen-year-old bride's dark black eyes and hair, and "the classic cast of her features," suggested "some Greek heroine of Byron's poems."[25] Thus in 1896 did their admiring son describe both George and Eliza as Greek in appearance.

Colvocoresses's second wife, Adeline Maria Swasey, whom he married on July 29, 1863, a year after Eliza's death, also had

[22]Ibid., p. 70.
[23]Ibid., p. 80.
[24]Ibid., pp. 70f., 183.
[25]Ibid., p. 97.

Norwich connections. She was a younger sister of Mrs. Alden Partridge, the sister-in-law of his benefactor.

Except for the three years (1858-61) spent at the Navy Yard in Portsmouth, New Hampshire, a "neat cottage" on one acre of land near the center of Norwich was home for the Colvocoresseses family until Eliza's death (August 23, 1862). The "cottage" was "improved and adorned" as the head of the family returned, on leave after sea-duty. It was a "bright and happy home."[26] Three of the four children of George and Eliza were born in Norwich: George Partridge (April 3, 1847), Franka Eliza (August 19, 1850), named for her paternal grandmother and for her mother; and Eva Freelon (July 19, 1853). The youngest child, Ellena Seaman, was born at Portsmouth (July 8, 1859).

Around 1865-66 the Norwich home was sold. Colvocoresses then bought a house in Litchfield, Connecticut, a community with good schools for his three daughters. His descendants still own this large, imposing house on the Litchfield green.

When the sixteen-year-old Greek immigrant entered the United States Navy as a midshipman early in 1832, he embarked on a career which enjoyed status. He joined a proud professional elite drawn exclusively from the upper classes of American society. Naval officers' messes, a contemporary remarked, "were seasoned with a strong smell of aristocracy."[27] During the four years of the United States Exploring Expedition (1838-42) Colvocoresses's messmates included a Lee from Virginia; a Pinkney from Maryland; a Gansevoort from New York; an Alden from Massachusetts; the sons of naval heroes, governors and important political figures.

Until the Academy at Annapolis was established in 1845, naval officers received on-the-job training. Midshipmen for six years, they went on cruises and spent one or two years on "receiving-ships" in navy yards where professors prepared them for examinations. While on his first Mediterranean cruise aboard the frigate *United States,* Midshipman Colvocoresses visited his

[26]Ibid., p. 99.

[27]W. Stanton, *The Great United States Exploring Expedition of 1838-1842* (Berkeley, Los Angeles and London, 1975), p. 69. For the discussion of the Expedition I have relied mainly on Stanton and *Magnificent Voyagers,* eds. H. J. Viola and C. Margolis (Washington, D.C., 1985).

parents and relatives on Chios.[28] A decade later, on a second Mediterranean cruise Lieutenant Colvocoresses did not have the same "pleasure," his ship going only as far as Malta.

The distance between Chios and Vermont notwithstanding, family ties were maintained. In 1849 they were renewed by the visit of Colvocoresses's brother Stamati.[29] The visitor spent some time in Norwich and taught French. Having lived in England, Stamati Calvocoresses spoke good English. One wonders how much Greek Colvocoresses had left in 1849, after 26 years' residence in the United States and without Greek contacts. The two brothers probably spoke English to each other.

At the end of six years as midshipman, Colvocoresses was ordered to Baltimore to be examined for promotion. "This was one of the most important events of my life, as it was to decide whether I should remain in the Navy."[30] On June 28, 1838, the successful candidate was promoted to "passed midshipman." Thus once again Baltimore was a propitious turning point in his life. President Martin Van Buren signed the warrant.

Two months later (August 18, 1838), Passed Midshipman Colvocoresses set sail from Hampton Roads, Virginia, on the US Brig *Porpoise*. One of the 54 carefully selected officers of the United States Exploring Expedition commanded by Lieutenant Charles Wilkes, he experienced the dangers and thrills of the epic cruise that established the young republic, his adopted country, as a world-class naval power and leader in scientific exploration.

The expedition's youthful "gentlemen" officers, including Colvocoresses, collected thousands of artifacts and specimens of flora and fauna from around the world. Under broiling suns they measured oceans, mapped the skies, surveyed new lands and charted vast areas of dangerous seas. Some of their Pacific charts were used in World War II. Twice risking their lives in the ice-bound waters at the bottom of the earth, they proved the existence of another continent which they named *Antarctica*. There and in many other remote places they left their names, mementoes of their courage and professionalism.

[28]Whether the visit occurred in 1832 or in 1837 is not clear: *Narrative*, p. 41 and Appendix I and *Records*, p. 82.

[29]*Records*, p. 99.

[30]*Narrative*, p. 41.

The officers also kept daily journals, ordered by their commander and examined by him regularly. Of these, twenty are extant, deposited in various libraries. On the basis of his journal Colvocoresses published a book in New York in 1852. Its long title, typical of that time, summarizes the contents: *Four Years Madeira-Cape Verd Islands-Brazil-Coast of Patagonia-Chile-Peru-Paumato Group-Society Islands-Navigator Group-Australia-Antarctic Continent-New Zealand-Friendly Islands-Fejee Group-Sandwich Islands-Northwest Coast of America-Oregon-California-East Indies-St. Helena, &c., &c.* The journal and the book manuscript are in Yale's Western Americana Collection.

On the title-page the author identifies himself as "Lieut. Geo. M. Colvocoresses, U.S. Navy, An Officer of the Expedition." In the brief preface he expresses hope that the "general reader" will find his work has "the merit of being instructive and entertaining, concise and cheap." His hopes were not in vain. The book went into five editions in three years.

Unlike Odysseus of Ithaca, Colvocoresses of Chios wrote his own odyssey, 371 pages long. In a generally plain style he tells the fascinating story of a young Greek American naval officer on the greatest adventure of his life. In addition to an account of the exploring and scientific activities of the Expedition, Colvocoresses describes the many places he visited and the peoples he encountered during a spectacular voyage which took almost four years to circumnavigate the globe.

On this voyage he observed an endless variety of institutions, human behavior and cultures.[31] He noted that in Brazil racial prejudice was less strong "than among us." On Tonga, Christian natives proved to be the troublemakers rather than the pagans. On the Fiji Islands he was eyewitness of an attempt to kidnap women for "cannibal purposes." He accepted the idea of the white man's burden, concluding that the Fijians would be better off if they were conquered by the "United States or some other civilized nation." Colvocoresses was always curious and observant,

---

[31]Colvocoresses, *Four Years*, pp. 31, 128, 144, 166, 184. In 1925, the author's grandson and namesake was given the copy presented (March 23, 1852) by his grandfather to Captain Partridge, in Norwich, Vermont. In May 1930 he wrote on the first fly-leaf: "Very interesting & instructive with excellent descriptions of many places which I have visited from 1902 to date & seen the changes in them that my Grandfather would not believe possible, G. M. C."

the perfect tourist. In Honolulu, "that New York" of the Pacific, he "visited every object worthy of notice." Much of what he saw and described no longer exists.

Midshipman Colvocoresses described women at length, commenting on their status, appearance, virtues and faults. He found the ladies of Lima to be "handsome, but their minds are neglected, nor are their morals what they should be." Fijian women were faithful to their brutal husbands. Some of them were skilled in surgery and "midwifery, a distinct profession." In the Pacific Northwest he saw an Indian tribe whose women were "very good-looking," and another with "not very good-looking" women who were worked like slaves. The "Chief Squaw" of the Sachal tribe impressed him favorably as "a woman of great energy and character," superior to most men.[32]

Descriptions of nature are frequent.[33] The trees of Tahiti "literally alive with songsters of every plumage imaginable." The icebergs of Antarctica, a "magnificent spectacle" of masses, "assuming the shape of a Gothic church, with arched windows and doors." Mounts Rainier and Olympus, "a magnificent picture . . . as the rising sun illumined their lofty peaks, and dispersed the mists that still floated in fleecy clouds over the tranquil valleys around their bases."

The history-making expedition ended July 3, 1842. After six months of leave, Colvocoresses was posted to Boston to the "Receiving Ship" *Ohio*. He remained there until ordered as "Master" of the USS *Warren*, bound for the Pacific. While on this tour of duty he was commissioned lieutenant (December 7, 1843). In that capacity he served on the schooner *Shark* and the store-ship *Relief*. Returning to the United States on April 14, 1846, he married Eliza Halsey in New York City four weeks later. The bride's uncle, Rev. Charles Halsey, officiated at the wedding ceremony in St. George's Chapel.[34]

The second Mediterranean cruise (1847-49) was followed by service on the African coast (1851-52). On his return from the African cruise, Colvocoresses enjoyed 18 months with his

[32]Ibid., pp. 59, 178, 180, 233, 235, 242f.
[33]Ibid., pp. 76, 112, 232.
[34]*Records*, p. 83.

family in Norwich, "the longest 'leave' I ever had."[35] From 1853-55 he was stationed in New York. During this time his little son, George Partridge, was initiated into naval life. Staying with his father aboard the *North Carolina* for several weeks, he was cared for by Manuel, Colvocoresses's Italian servant and by "an old marine."[36]

From 1855-58 Colvocoresses served as executive officer on the US sloop-of-war *Levant* in the East Indian Squadron. His ship participated in the bombardment and capture of the four "Barrier Forts" near Canton (November 24-December 4, 1856).[37] Surprisingly tough Chinese resistance caused casualties and damages to the *Levant*. Colvocoresses expressed pride in this action, "an affair which will compare favorably with any achievement gained by the Navy during the War of 1812." This time, however, Americans aided the British, proving, in the British admiral's words, that "blood is thicker than water."

After a "pleasant voyage of 120 days" from Hong Kong, the *Levant* arrived at Boston (April 7, 1858). Colvocoresses then joined his family still residing in Norwich. In September he was ordered to the Navy Yard in Portsmouth, New Hampshire.

So often separated, this navy family had three final years together. "My family accompanied me, and the sojourn was a very agreeable one to us all."[38] Admiral Colvocoresses offers us a rare glimpse of our naval officer as *pater familias*. "We were under strict discipline and brought up in the old fashioned way."[39] The two older children, George Partridge and Franka Eliza, had daily lessons from their father, there being no school at the Navy Yard.

The outbreak of the Civil War put an end to this happy domestic period. On June 20, 1861, Colvocoresses was posted to New York to take command of the store-ship *Supply,* bound for Hampton Roads to join the Blockading Squadron.[40] Two months

[35]*Narrative*, p. 46.
[36]*Records*, p. 101.
[37]*Narrative*, pp. 46-60. The article by a grandson is based on these pages: Major Harold Colvocoresses, U.S. Marine Corps (Retired), "The Capture and Destruction of the Barrier Forts," *United States Naval Institute Proceedings* 64 (1938), pp. 680-684.
[38]*Narrative*, p. 64.
[39]*Records*, p. 111.
[40]*Narrative*, p. 65.

later (August 5) at Hampton Roads, he received promotion to commander, a rank attained by very few officers of foreign birth.[41] His fourteen-year-old son, George Partridge, was appointed his clerk.[42] Eliza and the three girls left Portsmouth and returned to the "cottage" in Norwich. A year later Eliza died at the age of 35, leaving Colvocoresses a widower with four children ranging in age from 3 to 15. On the day of his wife's death (August 23, 1862) he sailed from New York for the war-zone in the South.

Colvocoresses served throughout the Civil War.[43] From 1861-63 he commanded the store-ship *Supply,* making trips up and down the Atlantic Coast to supply the Federal blockade. On January 29, 1862, he captured a British schooner carrying arms and stores for the Confederacy. Because the case involved points of international law, it was later cited in text books. When the vessel and cargo were sold in New York, $127,395.56 were distributed among the officers and crew. Colvocoresses received $19,109.33 and his son, $2,229.43.[44]

From 1863 to September 1864, Colvocoresses commanded the sail-sloop *Saratoga,* attached to the South Atlantic Squadron, operating off the coast of Georgia.[45] On August 2, 1864, he organized and carried out the first of three raids into Confederate territory. Admiral Dahlgren, the squadron commander, praised him for this action in a general order, read on all the ships. That same month Dahlgren inspected the *Saratoga* and expressed to Colvocoresses his "satisfaction at the excellent condition of your ship." The admiral also recommended to the other commanders in the squadron Colvocoresses's method of protecting his ship from torpedo attacks.

[41]Ibid., p. 66. The autobiographical sketch ends with the words "I served as a Lieutenant eighteen years." He had waited a long time. E. Lonn, *Foreigners in the Union Army and Navy* (Baton Rouge, 1951), p. 630, comments that Colvocoresses "attained this rank only after many years in lower position." See also G. P. Perros, *Officers of Greek Descent in the Union Navy* (Washington, D.C., 1964), pp. 1-3.

[42]*Records,* p. 112.

[43]*Records,* pp. 112-157. Admiral Colvorcoresses meticulously documents his father's service in the Civil War, incorporating naval records, letters and newspaper accounts.

[44]Ibid., pp. 119-122.

[45]Ibid., pp. 126-157. A detailed account of this period. George Partridge served as his father's clerk on this ship. Steve Frangos has informed me that the ship's cook was a Greek and that the crew included two other Greeks as well.

A second expedition (August 16) was reported by Dahlgren to Secretary of the Navy Gideon Welles. (Like Colvocoresses, Welles was an alumnus of Norwich Academy.) "The activity and skill manifested by Captain Colvocoresses is entitled to the highest commendation and I shall give him another and a wider field for his labors."

After the third successful expedition, deep into enemy territory (August 26), Secretary of the Navy Welles sent Colvocoresses a letter of thanks for his "zealous and good service to the country."

While planning a fourth attack, Colvocoresses received orders to take command of the USS *Tuscarora* at Baltimore. The prospects of a "wider field of action" promised by Dahlgren never materialized. The unexpected transfer had been made without consultation with Admiral Dahlgren, who protested to Welles the transfer of Colvocoresses and requested in vain that the *Tuscarora* be assigned to his squadron.[46] Before Colvocoresses left the squadron, Admiral Dahlgren wrote to him, "I cannot permit you to depart without expressing my sense of your good service in this quarter, and with my best wishes."[47]

On September 29, 1864, Commander Colvocoresses boarded the USS *Wabash*, bound for New York. Severe storms on the voyage north made her captain seasick. Colvocoresses then took command.[48] The Greek-born naval officer was never seasick.[49]

The assignment to the *Tuscarora* was shortlived and Colvocoresses was ordered to Boston to command the USS *Dacotah*. Detached from it, he next commanded the USS *Wachusett*. On February 17, 1865, Colvocoresses received his final command, the sloop *St. Marys* on the Pacific Station. This sailing craft had originally been built to suppress the slave trade on the African coast.[50]

Among his father's papers, Admiral Colvocoresses found a letter addressed to the Navy Secretary. For the first time,

[46]Ibid., pp. 155-157.
[47]Ibid., pp. 155f.
[48]Ibid., p. 158.
[49]Ibid., p. 114. George Partridge recalled that once when he had been "wretchedly" seasick, "My father could not appreciate my condition as he had never been sea-sick."
[50]Ibid., p. 160.

Colvocoresses requested a change of orders. His disappointment is palpable, "My twenty years of service at sea, my character, which has enabled me without any extraneous influence to pass all the Retiring Boards, my behavior in this Rebellion . . . and my desire to be kept actively employed, have made me hope that the Department would feel disposed, this time, to give me a more desirable command."[51] The request was not granted.

Colvocoresses commanded the *St. Marys* on the west coast of South America until 1867. On one occasion, his prompt and decisive action not only protected American lives and property, but also saved the city of Valparaiso from bombardment by the Spanish fleet.[52] Colvocoresses had warned the Spanish admiral that although the *St. Marys* was not a powerful ship, she represented a great nation.

A final greater disappointment awaited him on his return from South America. A naval board in Philadelphia advanced Colvocoresses to the rank of captain and placed him on the retired list. When his career came suddenly to an end, he was 51 years old, with 35 years of service in the United States Navy.

Admiral Colvocoresses believed that great injustice had been done his father both during and after the war, that he had never received the commands he deserved. He speculated why, despite his excellent record, Colvocoresses had "received so little consideration" from naval authorities.[53]

For one thing, Captain Colvocoresses disdained self-promotion: he had "never courted political and personal influence and was too modest to assert his own merit."[54] For another, Colvocoresses's political views probably militated against him: "My father had always been a democrat, and although perfectly loyal to the government, he did not hesitate to freely express his opinion about persons and parties." On slavery, states-rights and other issues of the day, he "talked imprudently."[55] But there was another strike against him.

[51]Ibid., pp. 158f.
[52]Ibid., p. 160.
[53]Ibid., pp. 158-160. The intervening decades had not lessened the son's indignation over the unfair treatment meted out to his father.
[54]Ibid., p. 117.
[55]Ibid., pp. 117f. This suggests that Colvocoresses may have been a Southern sympathizer. If so, his political outlook had probably been influenced by the

Admiral Colvocoresses also believed that "narrow national prejudice" had been a decisive factor, "For even in this democratic and cosmopolitan country, a foreigner by birth and name . . . is apt to be regarded with disfavor in matters of preferment."[56] When the Greek immigrant's son wrote these lines, he himself had been an officer in the Navy for three decades. Thus he was not unaware of the elitism and aristocratic bias that have traditionally characterized that service.

When he was summarily retired in 1867, Captain Colvocoresses had lived 44 of his 51 years in the United States. It is very likely that in 1867 Greece, the land of his birth, would have seemed a foreign country to him. He had been educated in a famous American military academy. He had a 35-year record of exemplary service in the Navy of his adopted country. When in command, he had read the services of the Episcopal Church to the officers and crew of his ship.[57] His four children were ninth-generation Americans on their mother's side. His son was a midshipman at the Naval Academy at Annapolis. Nevertheless, George Musalas Colvocoresses may have always been thought to be not an American but rather a Greek, defined both by place of birth and by his foreign-sounding, polysyllabic surname.

The auspicious circumstances of his arrival and reception in this country in 1823-24 should have been prologue to an immigrant success story. It seems, however, to have turned out otherwise. Contrary to popular mythology, immigration to America does not automatically and inevitably guarantee acceptance, success or happiness.

For the remaining five years of his life, Captain Colvocoresses, USN (Retired) lived quietly in Litchfield, Connecticut, with his second wife and three daughters. On the night of June 3, 1872, while walking to the Bridgeport wharf to take a nightboat for New York, where he had a business appointment the next day, Colvocoresses was murdered by a thief.[58] Police reported that he had been shot through the heart with an old-fashioned Irish

Southerners with whom he had gone to school at the Academy in Norwich and with whom he had served in the Navy.

[56]Ibid., p. 118.

[57]Ibid., p. 99: "He made no pretensions in religious matters but held them in respect."

[58]Ibid., pp. 164-168.

dueling pistol. His hat, wig[59] and shattered bamboo sword-cane lay near his body. His satchel had been opened and its contents stolen. Colvocoresses's murderer was never identified. His insurance company claimed the death was a suicide, forcing the family into a long, costly and bitter legal contest.

His son noted the irony of his father's violent death. Captain Colvocoresses "had escaped one of the bloodiest massacres known to history as a child, been subject to the perils of flood and shore in every clime from a youth up, participated in two wars without injury and finally perished by the hand of an unknown assassin in the streets of a New England town."[60]

His funeral was held in St. Michael's Episcopal Church in Litchfield and he was buried in East Litchfield Cemetery.

Born in Chios and baptized a Greek Orthodox, Captain Colvocoresses died in Connecticut as an Episcopalian. An obelisk erected in 1875 marks his grave in the family plot.

George Musalas Colvocoresses appears to be the only one of the group that came between 1823 and 1828 to found a family which still exists in the United States. Moreover, he established a tradition of military careers for the men of his family. Three generations have followed his example. His son, George Partridge Colvocoresses (1847-1932), received an appointment from President Lincoln to the Naval Academy, from which he graduated in 1869. After 45 years of distinguished service, he retired with the rank of rear-admiral. The admiral's son, Harold Colvocoresses, also attended the Naval Academy and became an officer in the Marine Corps. Colonel Alden Partridge Colvocoresses (named for the benefactor of the family patriarch), great-grandson of the Greek immigrant, grandson of the admiral and son of George Musalas Colvocoresses, is a retired officer of the United States army.

Nor has the family forgotten the naval tradition begun in 1832 by Midshipman George M. Colvocoresses. This year, 1989, 166 years after the little immigrant from Chios disembarked from the *Margarita* in Baltimore, a great-great-great-granddaughter bearing the long name of her Greek ancestor

[59]Ibid., p. 97. He had lost his hair after a bout of yellow fever contracted while serving on the African coast, and wore a wig for the rest of his life.
[60]Ibid., p. 168.

has applied for admission to the Naval Academy. If appointed, she will become the fourth Midshipman Colvocoresses, a most worthy descendant of the first.

The Greek Pilgrims:
Tsakonas and Tsintzinians

PETER W. DICKSON

One testimony to the great importance of Theodore Saloutos's celebrated work, *The Greeks in the United States,* is that it is a gold mine of information about the early presence of Greeks in this country even though Saloutos himself was not able or inclined to pursue all the rich veins in this treasury of knowlelge. Perhaps the most extraordinary but almost totally unexplored story in Greek American history centers around the first wave of immigrants whom Saloutos called the "Greek Pilgrims." He was referring specifically to the beginning of mass migration in the 1880s from the area around Sparta in southern Greece. More broadly, Saloutos intended to refer also to immigrants from the central Peloponnese—the Arcadians—who began to follow the Spartans to America in the early 1890s. Both the Spartans and the Arcadians together constituted the foundation for the Greek community in this country, although to call them "Pilgrims" is a bit misleading because religious persecution was not a motivating factor in their decision to come to the New World.

Saloutos, nonetheless, makes another startling assertion that this mass migration was triggered by the actions of one pivotal figure—Christos Tsakonas from a village called Zoupena just a few miles southeast of Sparta. To attribute such a central role to one man for Greek mass migration is a bold hypothesis and there are no parallel claims regarding the migration patterns for the Irish, German, Italian, Jewish, Scandinavian, and Slavic ethnic groups. Yet Saloutos in fact makes such a claim when he writes:

Triggering the initial outflow of immigrants from Sparta was an obscure young man named Christos Tsakonas, born in 1848 in the village of Zoumpaina (ed. Zoupena). This "Christopher Columbus of Sparta" displayed the attributes of many of his contemporaries who were to emigrate. After completing two years in the village grammar school, Tsakonas set out for Piraeus in quest of a job. Making little headway there, he left for Alexandria, Egypt, where after encountering similar experiences he decided in 1873 to leave for America. At this time it was unusual for a man of peasant stock to seek his fortune in the New World. Tsakonas found the United States to his liking. After a brief visit in Greece in 1875, he left again for America, but this time in the company of five compatriots. *This group seems to have constituted the nucleus for the succeeding waves of immigrants from Sparta.*[1]

A bit later, Saloutos states that 12 to 15 Greeks left for America from the village of Tsintzina in 1877 and that some 70 more left from the same general area for Piraeus where they boarded three boats for America in the spring of 1882.

Saloutos did not follow up the story hidden behind this data. If he had, he would have uncovered not just the most extraordinary story in Greek American history but one of the most remarkable in the long history of migration to America. Indeed, these isolated fragments of information are the mere surface of the fantastic achievements of Christos Tsakonas, who directly and indirectly lured nearly 1,000 young Spartans to Chicago in the 1870s and 1880s. Saloutos did not realize that Tsakonas was actually born in Tsintzina—a secluded village in the heart of the Parnon mountain range northeast of Sparta—and that the first waves of immigrants in the late 1870s and early 1880s were almost exclusively from this one village.[2] The failure to ap-

[1]Saloutos, Theodore, *The Greeks in the United States* (Cambridge: Harvard University Press, 1964), p. 24.

[2]The Parnon mountain range comprises a large part of the eastern Peleponnese. Historically, the region has been known as "Tsakonia," where a distinct dialect was long spoken. After the creation of the modern Greek state in the 1830s, the northern and eastern section of Tsakonia were incorporated into the state of Ar-

preciate the degree to which migration was concentrated in one core group was due to the fact that the Tsintzinians after the Greek Revolution could be found in *three* villages—the original Parnon mountain retreat now used only as a resort during the hot summer months and two villages in the Evrotas valley: Goritsa and Zoupena, where Tsakonas's family resided most of the year. This phenomenon of double or multiple residences is not uncommon in mountainous parts of the Greek mainland and is called *diplokatoikia.*

The historical contribution of Tsakonas and his band of Spartans from Tsintzina and a few other neighboring villages such as Vasaras, Krysapha, Agriannos, Geraki, Arachova, Vamvakou, etc. is profound. These early pioneers founded the first Greek societies in both Chicago and San Francisco in the late 1880s. In the process, these two societies, especially the one in Chicago which established the city's first Greek Orthodox church in 1891, served as a model for the same institutional development in New York City. Furthermore, the Tsintzinians and their *patriotes* made their presence felt in Los Angeles and even the Hawaiian islands in the mid-1880s as fruit merchants and suppliers of produce for a chain of some 10 candy and fruit stores—the Greek American Fruit Company—that Tsakonas opened in eastern Ohio and western Pennsylvania in the 1880s.

This monumental achievement helped popularize the fruit and candy store business for later Greek immigrants. Indeed, the Tsintzinians, other Spartans, and the Arcadians by the mid-1890s had largely taken over the wholesale fruit business from the Italians in Chicago barely more than a decade following Tsakonas's own example of selling both fruit and candy in his first stores in Milwaukee in 1882. In no other line of business were the Greeks better established throughout America early in the twentieth century than the confectionary trade. By the 1920s there were more than 300 Greek-owned ice cream parlors in Chicago alone.

Even more amazing is that these early Tsintzinian pioneers and their descendants have held reunions for more than 90 years

cadia. The west and southwestern slopes of the Parnon fell under the administration of Laconia. Several families from this mountain region bear the name "Tsakonas," which is no guarantee of a direct blood relationship.

and since 1920 have gathered at their own private clubhouse on the shores of Lake Chautauqua near Jamestown, New York. This strong social or tribal bond is quite extraordinary. Indeed, it is unique in American cultural history for there appears to be no other group of people from one village anywhere that has continued to meet more than a century after arriving in America.

Saloutos provides the key details of the journey of these early Greek immigrants in a precise and systematic manner. Saloutos had only one source of information about Tsakonas—an article on early Laconian immigrants written by Nicholas Rozakos and published in *Nea Estia* in 1951. Rozakos (1908-1989) was originally from the Sparta area and familiar with the Tsintzinians, particularly those families which settled in San Francisco and Hawaii in the 1880s. A member of one of these families—an Athenian lawyer named Lycourgos Kamarinos—had given Rozakos a copy of the letter that Tsakonas wrote the night before he left Alexandria, Egypt, for America in February 1873. This letter, combined with information from Greek and American newspapers of the 1880s and 1890s, essays from Tsintzinian convention yearbooks (*lefkomata*), and data from passenger ship records in the National Archives in Washington, DC, document the emergence of the Greek community in America between 1873 and 1891.

Christos Tsakonas: The Greek Moses

Born in a tent in Tsintzina, Christos Tsakonas had the unfortunate fate of never knowing his father, also named Christos, who died shortly before his birth. His mother struggled against poverty in trying to raise two sons and two daughters. Tsakonas was greatly influenced by his mother's hardship. It appears to have shaped his character because his legendary stature among the early Spartan immigrants rested on his extraordinary degree of self-sacrifice and generosity in helping these young men. An article in the 1941 Tsintzinian convention yearbook stressed the importance of Tsakonas's childhood years in this remote mountain village "where hardships disciplined his character and a mother's self-sacrifice planted in him the seeds of unselfishness."[3] In the early 1860s, at the age of 14, Tsakonas decided to strike out on his own. He left Tsintzina for Piraeus and Athens where he worked in coffee shops. This line of work, however, did not satisfy his desire for something more substantial.

As Rozakos and Saloutos note, Tsakonas decided to try his luck in Egypt and, according to one account, he may have traveled there in the company of other Tsintzinians—especially those from the Andritsakis family who eventually became extraordinarily wealthy as cotton merchants. Tsakonas tried his hand as a money-changer but did not fare as well. In his letter dated 1 February 1873 to his brother Demitrios still living in Zoupena, Tsakonas declares that he intends to leave for "California" the next day with another young man named Nikolaos Anagnostou whom he has persuaded to join him. Anagnostou was from the Arcadian village of Achouria near Tripoli. It is very appropriate that from the first moment Tsakonas turned his thoughts to America, an Arcadian was beside him. This captures the essential unity of the Spartan-Arcadian exodus to the United States, even though the initial departure point in this unusual case happened to be Egypt.

Tsakonas and Anagnostou arrived in New York City on March 5, 1873, on a twin-masted steamship named the *Anglia*. At this time, there were only about 400 Greeks in all of North America, with most of them being sailors and a few merchants in the port cities of New Orleans, San Francisco, Boston and New York. The 1870 federal census for Chicago lists only 10 Greeks. This gives a baseline from which to appreciate the dramatic growth in the number of Greeks there after Tsakonas sensed that the city's reconstruction following the Great Fire of August 1871 offered great opportunities for poor but enterprising immigrants.

Compared to the other large European immigrant groups, those few Greeks who preceded Tsakonas to America had not yet begun to form societies or churches—the institutional framework that enables a *colony* of immigrants to transform itself into a more vibrant ethnic *community*. The sole exception

[3]See article entitled "Christ C. Chaconas" written by Peter Andreou of Chicago on pages 5-6 of the 1941 Tsintzinian convention yearbook.

was the small colony of Greek sailors and merchants in New Orleans where a Greek Orthodox Church served the spiritual needs of both Greek and non-Greeks beginning in 1866. However, this colony remained small for many years and did not enjoy substantial growth even after 1900 as Greeks tended to avoid the Deep South as a place to begin a new life.

Before setting down roots in Chicago, Tsakonas was shaped by his initial experiences in New York City. At that time, there were about only 40-50 Greeks there. Aside from the patrician Greek merchants in the area around Wall Street, only one Greek immigrant had made a mark in the city. He was Eleftherios Pilalas from the mountain village of Vresthena which is only a few miles from Tsintzina. Pilalas was the first Greek to open a candy store in America (around 1870) in the two hundred block of South Fifth Avenue. It would be logical to expect that Tsakonas learned the candy trade from Pilalas, but there is no evidence that they ever met. Unlike Tsakonas, who popularized this line of business, Pilalas never seems to have trained subsequent Greeks to sell candy and he certainly never encouraged Greeks to come to this country in any way compared to Tsakonas.

According to oral tradition preserved in writing in the 1927 Tsintzinian convention yearbook, Tsakonas's crucial encounter in New York was with Demitrios N. Botassis—one of the patrician merchants managing the Rallis firm and serving as consul in New York for the Greek government.[4] Tsakonas and his friend Anagnostou sought out assistance from Botassis, who was hostile to the idea of Greeks coming to America. Indeed, he insisted that the two young lads return immediately to the homeland where they were more badly needed. Botassis was strong-willed in his convictions and, as Saloutos makes clear, this Greek diplomat throughout the 1870s and 1880s worked closely with the Greek government and Athenian newspapers to discourage would-be immigrants by painting a gloomy picture of what America had to offer.

Tsakonas, however, would hear of none of this pessimism

[4]Much of the information about Tsakonas's encounter with Botassis is found in an article entitled "The Zupeena Pioneer" on pages 71-73 of the 1927 Tsintzinian convention yearbook. The author was Tsakonas's grand-nephew, James A. Chacona, who along with his own father—A. D. Chacona—took great care to preserve the history of Tsakonas's life in essays in the 1920s and 1930s.

and after a heated argument in Botassis's office, he finally persuaded the consul to at least give him some direction. According to tradition, Botassis obtained some candy supplies for Tsakonas and Anagnostou and got them started as peddlers on the street. If true, this momentous encounter between Tsakonas, a Peloponnesian peasant, and Botassis, a prototype of the young urban professional from Wall Street, had a decisive impact on Greek American history. It was the modest first step that Tsakonas took on his way to the creation of his celebrated chain of candy and fruit stores.

Whatver initial success Tsakonas had in New York, he clearly had on his mind traveling further west to California, and he evidently was headed there when he arrived in Chicago in 1873, where he again enjoyed extraordinary success as a fruit peddler. The benefits to his impoverished family back in Zoupena were obvious to others in the village when he returned in 1875 to retire some family debts. It was while he was in Greece that Tsakonas took the step that earned his claim to fame. Passenger ship records in the National Archives confirm that he returned to America in September 1875 along with five young men, as Rozakos had asserted. The fateful five were a nine-year old nephew, Christos Serafis; two cousins, Nikolaos Benekos and Ioannis Tsetseris; and two others from Zoupena, Nikolaos Politis and Nikolaos Tselekis. In luring these relatives and friends to Chicago, Tsakonas was not simply thinking of giving them a better future. He was also motivated by a desire for bodyguards. He had been drugged, beaten, and robbed in a hotel in Paris during his journey back to Greece. Whatever the motives, these five young men and Tsakonas were the nucleus of what Saloutos called the "succeeding waves" of immigrants from Sparta.

Chicago as a Model Greek Community

Tsakonas became famous not only for starting an exodus to a promised land, but also for setting in motion a process that was to give Chicago a central place in Greek American history. The "succeeding waves" of arrivals from Tsintzina were frequent and large enough to create the need for institutions and a church to preserve the interests, both cultural and religious, of the small Spartan colony in Chicago.

The turning point clearly occurred in 1882, as claimed by Spiridon Kontakis in his book *The Greeks in America,* published in 1906. In the spring of 1882 three Athenian newspapers (*Sphaira, Aeon,* and *Stoa*) noted the departure from Piraeus of nearly 100 people from Tsintzina and nearby villages for America. This phenomenon captured public attention because such an exodus to the New World was unprecedented given the traditional inclination of Greeks to try Egypt or Romania to improve their fortunes. Prior to 1882, only about 15-20 Greeks arrived per year in the port of New York. Yet in this fateful year, the number suddenly jumped to 126. The passenger ship records and Athenian newspaper articles confirm that at least 106 were from Tsintzina and a few other neighboring villages.

The surge in the numbers of Spartans in Chicago in the early 1880s eventually encouraged the development of a society (*eteria*) exclusively for Greeks. It is not surprising that the first such society in Chicago (and North America for that matter) was called the Therapnean Society. The name was taken from the name of the Demos Therapnon which included Tsintzina and six other villages on the southwestern slopes of the Parnon Mountains overlooking the Evrotas valley. There were of course other Greeks in Chicago from other parts of Laconia, but they were essentially all *patriotes* because most of them were from the Demos Oinountos (Vasaras-Krysapha) and the Demos Geronthrae (Geraki) which bordered on the Demos Therapnon, to the north and south respectively.

According to the research of Professor Andrew Kopan, this Spartan colony in the 1880s was largely concentrated on the near north side of the "Loop" close to the intersection of Clark and Kinzie Streets. This was in the heart of the commercial activity associated with the Water Street market place and these Spartans were in time to become major figures in their own right as major wholesalers of fruit and produce. The most famous was John Procos, who with his partner Christoforos Coumountzis helped create the Therapnean Society in 1887. Three or four years later the society was renamed the "Lycourgos Society" to broaden its appeal given the arrival of immigrants from the other townships in Laconia.

This tiny Spartan colony with its unique society was to become a model for institutional development elsewhere in America among early Greek immigrants. In July 1888, a year after the creation of the Therapnean Society in Chicago, another Tsintzinian named Demitrios G. Camarinos founded the first Greek society west of the Mississippi River. It was called the Hellenic Mutual Benevolent Society and served as a vehicle for protecting the interests of the Greeks working in San Francisco and later for raising funds to build the first local Greek Orthodox Church—Holy Trinity, which was dedicated in 1904.

Like Tsakonas, Camarinos was an almost mythical figure in his own right. A bon vivant, he enjoyed phenomenal success and widespread fame as a wholesale fruit merchant. As consul for the Greek government in San Francisco in 1892-1894, he solidified his reputation as the founding father of the Greek community of the Bay area. Nicholas Rozakos, in his historical research, suggested that Camarinos preceded Tsakonas to this country and that the latter probably was en route to California in 1873 to join Camarinos. However, Camarinos's obituary in January 1903 indicates that he arrived in America in 1877, perhaps as one of the 12-15 Tsintzinians Saloutos states came that year. There can be little doubt that Camarinos was in close contact with the Tsintzinians in Chicago because he supplied them with bananas and pineapples from Hawaii through his own export-import firm—the California Fruit Market—based in Honolulu. This enterprise in Honolulu was managed by Camarinos's brother and nephews, several of whom worked for Tsakonas in Chicago in the early 1880s before heading to the West Coast.[5]

The relationship between the small Tsintzinian-Spartan colony in Chicago and the emergence of an organized Greek community in New York City is a somewhat more complex story, but there is a clear historical connection. Kontakis states that the visibility

[5]The professional and social bond between those Tsintzinians in Hawaii and those on the mainland remained strong despite the separation and passage of time. The most famous Greek in Hawaii—George Lycourgos—took his daughter to the 1925 Trintzinian convention for the dedication of the lakeside clubhouse in the presence of the Greek ambassador. Other Spartans from Hawaii in the late 1940s visited the famous clubhouse where hula dances were performed for entertainment.

of Greeks in Manhattan by the early 1880s was fading, even though it never was much to speak of from the start. Some of the Greek mercantile firms that first emerged in the 1850s and 1860s were still present in the financial section around Wall Street. But relative to the huge influx of immigrants from Ireland, Germany, and Italy, the numbers of Greeks in New York hardly changed at all between the 1860 and the 1880 federal census, with the latter listing only 69 Greeks. By 1890, New York had about 250-300 Greeks but there still were no Greek societies or churches. In contrast, the Greek community in Chicago by 1890 was at least as large, if not larger, and had its own society with plans to bring a priest from the old country to head an exclusively *Greek* Orthodox Church.

The Greeks in New York did eventually take the first steps toward institutional formation—a society and church—but this development was directly influenced by the actions of the Tsintzinians and other Spartans already established in Chicago. Evidence for this claim is the role of Greece's Prince George— the second son of King George I—who on a world tour from the Far East to America passed through San Francisco, Chicago, and New York in the summer of 1891. As a handsome 22-year old, he had become an international celebrity overnight for saving the life of the Russian czarevitch Nicholas during an assassination attempt in Japan. Though few in number, Greeks in these American cities turned out to greet Prince George at railroad stations or at the hotels where he was lodged.

The origin of the Greek community of New York dates from this event, specifically the last day of the visit of Prince George when he met with a group of representatives from the local Greek "colony." According to Thomas Fairchild in *The Greeks in America* (1913), it was at this meeting that the Prince urged the New York Greeks to form a society and church. The meeting took place at the Prince's hotel, the Brevoort House, on the afternoon of July 3 only a few hours before he boarded a ship for Europe to complete his round-the-world tour.

The basis for Prince George's recommendation is clear. Contemporary accounts of his tour in the American newspapers confirm that his advice to the hitherto unorganized Greeks in New York was based on his experience at Union Station in Chicago on June 29 when the Tsintzinians and other Spartans greeted him with a 35-man band.[6] The welcome amazed him as he had received no such formal reception from the Greeks in San Francisco. The band and society leaders escorted him down Michigan Avenue to his room at the Auditorium Hotel. The Prince, who was trying to travel incognito, later remarked to a New York journalist that this warm welcome gave his trip a public character that he had not sought. Nonetheless, his half-day stay in Chicago clearly influenced his subsequent advice to the embryonic Greek community of New York. Shortly after the prince's departure, the New York Greeks formed the Brotherhood of Athena which, in turn, took steps to establish a Greek Orthodox Church in 1892—Holy Trinity. That church, now a cathedral, enjoys the status of being the second oldest parish in *continuous* existence in North America (after the one founded in New Orleans in the 1860s).

Another important factor had a major impact on the emergence of an organized Greek community in New York during the summer of 1891. The Greek prince fortuitously had arrived only a few weeks after the largest influx of Greeks into New York—some 499 on five boats from late April through the month of May. All these young Greeks were from the Sparta region. Nearly 90 were from Tsintzina alone and another 120 from Geraki, a large town only 4 miles from Zoupena where Tsakonas's family resided.

This was the largest exodus of Greeks from one small area up to that time and it is doubtful that it has ever been equaled. All the Tsintzinians were headed directly for Chicago to join in the formation of the new parish—Annunciation. Among those Spartans staying in New York, many undoubtedly turned out to greet Prince George when his train arrived in Grand Central Station on the evening of June 30. It is unlikely that the Prince realized that his compatriots had just arrived in America; but Botassis, the consul who had crossed swords with Tsakonas exactly 18 years earlier, was certainly aware of the inexorable tide of

---

[6]The evidence for the 35-man Tsintzinian band escorting Prince George is drawn from an article in the 1942 Tsintzinian convention yearbook and numerous accounts in Chicago and New York newspapers, especially the July 1, 1891, issue of *The World,* which had hired a journalist to interview the prince on the train ride to New York.

immigrants from the Sparta region. At this point, there was little he could do to stem this development. In this sense, the exodus of 1891 represents the triumph of "Barba" Christos Tsakonas and his tribe over the headstrong aristocratic merchant from Spetses.

The Market Collapse for Greek Currants

The foregoing historical reconstruction of the early years of the Greek communities in this country has several important implications for the historiography of Greek America. Perhaps the most important issue surrounds the conventional wisdom more or less accepted by Saloutos that the first wave of mass migration from the Peloponnese was directly linked to the collapse of the market in France for currants (small seedless grapes) cultivated in Greece. This cause-and-effect relationship has long seemed compelling because the importance of the export of currants to France, Russia, and other European countries for the Greek economy is not open to question. After the mid-1870s, currants were the principal source of foreign exchange for the kingdom of Greece.

This *heavy* emphasis on the impact of the market collapse is questionable in view of the new research on the Tsintzinians and other Spartans. All the developments in Chicago and New York just noted—including the large mass exodus in the spring of 1891—took place *before,* not after, the collapse in the market price for currants.

A close reading of Saloutos's secondary sources used in his main work, *The Greeks in the United States,* pinpoints the "break" in the market price as the spring of 1893. These sources, largely drawn from essays by prominent Greek politicians in the *Economic Journal* published in London, convey a picture of an economic calamity that unfolded very slowly even though the full implications of the disaster were there for all to see even before the market collapse in 1893. For example, the secondary sources indicate that a few astute observers in Athens were well aware of the long term implications when the French parliament began to impose the first tariffs and non-tariff barriers against the importation of currants from Greece in 1889-1890.

However, the inclination among most Greeks, especially the cultivators of the vines, was to dismiss this reality and to assume that market demand would remain strong despite brief fluctuations. Even after the full impact of the French embargo was felt in 1893, many Greeks developed a false sense of security when the Russians briefly took advantage of the depressed price for currants. By 1896-1897, the demand for Greek currants in Russia dropped suddenly in reaction to strong pressure in Bessarabia to protect the domestic wine industry, as was the case in France earlier.

The fact that the Greeks were slow to learn the lessons of this experience is reflected in uneven patterns of migration throughout the 1890s. It bobs up and down in an inconsistent manner at a relatively low level, never rising above a couple of thousand per year at most. Large-scale mass migration from the kingdom of Greece does not begin until 1902-1903, after which its surges dramatically. Thus, it appears that there was a significant "time lag" with respect to the full economic impact of the crisis in the international market for Greek currants.

Another fact that explodes the thesis of a cause-and-effect relationship between early Greek migration to America and the currant market is the absence of immigrants from the prime areas where the vines were grown in the late nineteenth century. For example, there is no evidence to show that those from Cephalonia, Zakinthos, and the northwestern part of the Peloponnese—Patras-Gastouni—were present in the wave of immigrants in the 1890s to any significant degree. The in-depth research of Professor Janeen Costas (University of Utah) underscores that farmers and workers from Cephalonia where the vine was grown extensively responded to market turndowns in the nineteenth century by migrating, but they only made their presence felt in America after 1900.[7]

Furthermore, the Spartan-Arcadian exodus to America could not have had a *direct* root in the collapse of the market for currants. This grape was not grown extensively in these two provinces which are largely mountainous. They were areas no doubt beset

[7]For more information about the migration to America from these grape-growing regions of Greece see: Costa Janeen Arnold, "The History of Migration and Political Economy of Rural Greece: A Case Study," *Journal of Modern Greek Studies*. Vol. 6, No. 2 (1988), pages 159-185.

with economic problems—the lack of fertile land, undercultiva-
tion, and a surplus labor force. These factors were at play certainly in Laconia, which was one of the poorest regions in Greece.
The critical variable, however, was the role assumed by Tsakonas.
In an essay written in 1941, he is described as luring "idle young
men from Tsintzina" to Chicago.[8] These idle young men reflected
the inability of the local Laconian economy to give them a
meaningful economic future in part because a "baby boom"
during the 1870s and 1880s was too great for the agricultural
economy to absorb. It is worth noting that in the Mani peninsula,
which is the most barren area in all of Greece, the same hardship conditions existed. The safety valve for that region was a
long established tradition of young Maniates finding employment in the Athens police force or in military careers—outlets
which were not traditional for the Tsintzinians and others from
the villages in the Parnon mountains.

The Tsintzinian Diaspora

The subsequent diaspora of the Tsintzinians and their *patriotes*
throughout American society is also significant. At a very early
date it helped establish a pattern of Greeks settling in small
towns in the Midwest as well as in a large metropolis such as
Chicago. Furthermore, the diaspora was in many respects a function or consequence of the success Tsakonas had with his chain
of candy and fruit stores—the Greek American Fruit Company.
The ability to succeed in this line of business in small towns was
demonstrated for other Greeks who followed and gave them a
viable option to urban ghettoes, such as Chicago's fabled "Greektown" along Halstead Street.

The diaspora of the Tsintzinians and their subsequent inclination to assimilate into the cultural-social environment of broader
American society was foreshadowed when Tsakonas established
his first candy and fruit stores in Milwaukee around 1882. He
took this momentous step at the same time that the large
Tsintzinian contingent arrived in Chicago. The factors behind
his decision to depart Chicago at such a pivotal moment are un-

[8]See Andreou, op cit, p. 5.

known. Whatever his motives, the diaspora of the Tsintzinians was built into his own behavior of migrating from town to town to establish stores that offered ready employment to the young Tsintzinians and Spartans who had been lured to America by stories about the fabulously successful "Barba Christos."

This dispersal of young Greeks throughout America was astonishingly widespread due to the transcontinental character of Tsakonas's commercial network. Two young Tsintzinians— Ioannis and Nikolaos Chronis—departed Chicago in 1884 for Los Angeles where they became the city's first Greek proprietors with a fruit store on Spring Street. They hired Chinese laborers to pick lemons and oranges which were subsequently supplied to Tsakonas's stores via Chicago. The Chronis brothers, however, did not make a permanent impact on the emergence of a Greek community in Los Angeles, returning to Greece in the mid-1890s following a costly failure in shipping lettuce by train to Chicago.

The situation was quite different with respect to the other branches of Tsakonas's farflung operations. As he moved from town to town opening his series of fruit and candy stores in the 1880s, he turned over the daily management of these enterprises to his young compatriots. In a sense, Tsakonas was a peripatetic figure—a pied piper of sorts—who created a commercial network generating new possibilities outside Chicago for other Greeks. Furthermore, his strategy of selecting smaller towns and cities with robust economies based on vibrant local industries made the area of eastern Ohio and western Pennsylvania a magnet for young Greek immigrants in the 1880s and 1890s. All stores in his Greek American Fruit Company were well situated to piggyback on local industrial development. It is no coincidence that his stores in Ohio, such as those in Akron and Youngstown as well as those in Pennsylvania—Titusville, Oil City, Sharon, and New Castle—all benefited from being in a region that was then the industrial heartland of America.

This strategic sense of Tsakonas was decisive because it created an attractive alternative for his followers, who might have stayed in Chicago where the economic situation was more competitive, especially once the Arcadians began to arrive in large numbers in the 1890s. More broadly, his popularization of the fruit and candy store business had far-reaching consequences because Greeks did not have to resign themselves to the kind of heavy manual labor associated with work in factories, mines, or on the railroads. In sum, Tsakonas played a central role in giving many Greek immigrants a good head-start in becoming shop-keepers in smaller Midwestern towns, which in turn fostered assimilation and quicker entry into the American middle class than would have been the case if they had stayed within the more sociologically restricted environment of an urban Greek ghetto.

The most exotic example of the enterprising and adaptive character of the Tsintzinians and other early Spartans who fol-lowed Tsakonas to Chicago can be found among those who migrated to the Hawaiian islands in the 1880s. The Camarinos brothers and their cousins and nephews from Tsintzina and the neighboring village of Vasaras demonstrated an extraordinary ability to succeed in commercial ventures and adjust to a non-western cultural environment despite the fact that most of these young Greek males were peasants with little or no education. Tsakonas's long-term influence as the model of the successful Greek entrepreneur in a non-Greek and pluralistic social environ-ment is underscored in the lives of those Tsintzinians and Spartans who laid the foundation for a Greek community in the middle of the Pacific Ocean.[9]

The Legacy of Tsakonas

Tsakonas has cast a long shadow on Greek American history. The magnitude of his stature was evident even to his contem-poraries, who were quite conscious of being part of a miniscule ethnic group. A measure of the debt these early Spartan im-migrants felt toward Tsakonas was apparent as early as 1895 when they honored him with a special birthday present at a banquet in Jamestown, New York. The present was a mortgage document on his home in Niles, Ohio, stamped "paid in full."

[9]Saloutos twice visited Hawaii and met with Helen Chapin, the foremost authority on the early Spartan settlers in the Hawaiian islands. Saloutos, however, was not aware of the close relationship between Tsakonas, the Tsintzinians, and these Hawaiian Greeks which is now more fully appreciated as a result of the collaborative research since August 1985 between the present author and Chapin.

Tsakonas broke down and cried on this occasion, but it was a fitting tribute to a man who had extended unusual generosity toward others all his life.

Tsakonas returned to his home village of Tsintzina in 1900. Following success in arranging new philanthropic projects to make life easier for his compatriots, he died sometime around 1909. Statues were later erected in Zoupena of Tsakonas and his life-long business partner, Ioannis Tsetseris, to commemorate their role as benefactors. For those Greeks he brought to America, it would be difficult to improve on the testimony contained in an article from the 1941 Tsintzinian convention yearbook which notes, "Uncle Christ died, but his deeds will be remembered. The Tsintzinians of *Greece* are reminded when they see his statue of a benefactor who raised their standard of living. More than one thousand *Americans* whose fathers or grandfathers were led by him to this prosperous land, enjoy advantages and opportunities that their ancestors never dreamed of."[10] The author of these words pleaded for the younger generations of Tsintzinians to preserve their Greek heritage. That later generations have continued the tradition of holding reunions for nearly 100 years is perhaps the greatest tribute to Tsakonas and his unparalleled influence on Greek American history.

The Tsakonas's legacy is unique and profound. He:

— singlehandedly triggered mass migration from the Sparta region in the 1870s and 1880s, which in turn encouraged Greeks from other parts of the Peloponnese (especially Arcadia) to come to America;

— established Chicago as a particularly advantageous city for the early Spartan and Arcadian immigrants to make their mark;

— made his influence felt through his *patriotes* who established the first exclusively Greek societies in North America in Chicago and San Francisco in 1887 and 1888, respectively;

[10]Author of this article was Peter Andreou, whose own father was among those lured to Chicago by Tsakonas in the late nineteenth century.

— encouraged exceptional entrepreneurial skill among his young followers, some of whom were the first Greeks in Los Angeles and Honolulu, where they succeeded in the fruit and produce business;

— created the first Greek-owned business franchise (the Greek American Fruit Company) which was also transcontinental and transoceanic in scope;

— popularized the fruit and candy store business among early Greek immigrants, who enjoyed a near monopoly with their confectionaries and ice cream parlors by 1920;

— demonstrated the success a Greek immigrant could have if he chose to open businesses in smaller towns or cities where industrial development was in full sway;

— stimulated a strong orientation toward the conservative social value system of the small shopkeeper in contrast to the outlook of a farmer or industrial laborer.

This last observation is perhaps the most important of all from the perspective of the historian or sociologist of the Greek American experience. Saloutos and later Professor Charles Moskos have emphasized that the most distinguishing characteristic of Greek Americans has been their persistent drive to enter the middle and upper-middle class of American society. The corresponding inclination to what is usually termed "bourgeois" is, of course, found in other American ethnic groups. Nonetheless, the strong desire of Greek Americans for economic advancement and social acceptance is predominant and among the earliest immigrants was no doubt reinforced by their conservative political traditions—nationalist and royalist—for which the region of Sparta and the Peloponnese generally were well-known.

In sum, the early Tsintzinians and Spartans fit the Saloutos-Moskos interpretation of the essential "bourgeois" orientation of Greek American culture. Indeed, one may postulate that these early pioneers were the paradigm for later immigrants. There were, no doubt, exceptions to the rule. It was the fate of many Greeks to work on the railroads, the mines in Utah, and factories in such milltowns as Lowell, Massachusetts. But the Tsintzinians and their Spartan compatriots set the model for success as middle-class shopkeepers who worked hard to enable their children to enjoy first-class educations in American schools. The Tsintzinians were not only the largest group of Greeks in America—over 3,000 in the 1920s and 1930s—but were widely recognized as among the richest and best educated. The ability of the Tsintzinian pioneers to place some of their sons in Ivy League universities before 1920 is the best evidence of their role as a model for other Greek immigrants and as originators of a pattern that has been characteristic of the Greek American experience ever since the early years of this century.

One final observation about the enduring impact of these "Mayflower" Greeks is perhaps worth advancing in terms of historiography. Dan Georgakas has warned rightly of the misleading tendency we have to "back fit" much of Greek American history based on more recent experiences. For example, there certainly was a darker underside to the early Greek American experience. The harsh "padrone" system of enforced servitude and economic exploitation was common in many businesses. Although Tsakonas through his personal example discouraged such abuses, it was not totally unknown among some of the more materialistic and aggressive Tsintzinian businessmen. Daily hardships were part and parcel even of the lives of those Greek immigrants relatively fortunate to work in a candy store or ice cream parlor as opposed to a mine or a factory. Their lives should not be romanticized.

On a broader level, caution must be exercised about "back fitting" data or assumptions about the early decades of Greek American history. The accomplishments of Tsakonas are so extraordinary and unique that patterns directly or indirectly associated with him might never have evolved. Had he decided to stay in Egypt, the Tsintzinians, other Spartans, and the Arcadians of the 1880s and 1890s probably would have never had any reason to think of America as a promised land. If these Pelopo. mesians had not been encouraged to migrate to places like Chicago, instead of 20,000 Greeks in America in the year

1900, there might have only been five hundred or a thousand unorganized Greeks with no societies or churches.

Without the unique phenomenon of "Barba" Christos Tsakonas, the Greeks would have lost more than twenty years in terms of institutional and social development, finding themselves even further behind other and significantly larger European immigrant groups. To be sure, America would still have been a magnet for impoverished Greeks after 1900 and these people eventually would have found means to make their way. However, it is not unreasonable to claim that their task was made easier by the paths cleared by those who came before them. In this respect, Tsakonas certainly deserves the title as the "Greek" Christopher Columbus bestowed on him by Saloutos, and his young Spartans were indeed the founding fathers of the Greek American community.

The Greeks of Hawaii

HELEN GERACIMOS CHAPIN

Introduction

The history of the Greeks of Hawaii is unique in the annals of the Greek diaspora throughout the world. A distance of 10,000 miles from Europe, the Hawaiian Islands are 2,700 miles from the nearest land mass and are the world's most isolated archipelago. The arrival of Greeks in Hawaii began soon after the British found their way there in 1778 and was well ahead of the entry of Greeks into the United States. An independent kingdom long before American annexation in 1898, Hawaii has served as a "distant magnet"[1] for Greek transients and then for settlers up to the present.

Although patterns of migration and settlement bear similarities to those into the U.S., there are differences worth noting. The colorful history of the Hawaii movement has more in common with patterns of migration and settlement into Hawaii itself. Its intense multicultural environment has hastened assimilation and acculturation, yet at the same time has fostered diversity and pluralism—a seeming paradox illustrated by the Greeks, who have successfully adapted but have maintained ethnic strength and exercised influence on Island history far beyond their numbers.

Greek history in Hawaii covers four distinct periods.[2] Briefly, the first period, from about 1800 to 1880, witnessed the arrival

[1]Philip Taylor, *The Distant Magnet: European Emigration to the U.S.A.* (London: Eyre & Spottiswoode, 1971). Regarding Hawaiian spelling, I am following the modern practice of including glottal stops and macrons which indicate pronunciation and meaning.

[2]See Helen G. Chapin, "The Queen's 'Greek Artillery Fire': Greek Royalists

55

and usually departure of a dozen or so sailors and drifters. Phases of Greek culture entered and took root—to identify only the most obvious, the name "Polynesia," or Greek for "many islands,"[3] to signify the vast watery triangle covering thousands of miles of Pacific Ocean and countless islands.

The second period, 1880 to 1900, saw the immigration of 50 or so men, principally from the Peloponnese, who became residents and set up small business enterprises. During this time the Hawaiian monarchy came under direct attack by American sympathizers. This culminated in the revolution that overthrew the legitimate government, a failed counterrevolution by Hawaiian nationalists, including the Greeks, and American annexation.

With the creation of the Territory of Hawaii in 1900, the history entered its third period, from 1900 to 1945. These years marked the formation of family life that gave permanence to the Greek presence. Men either returned to Greece or traveled to American cities for wives. A colony of up to 200 men, women, and children lived on two islands, Oahu and Hawaii (there are eight major islands in the chain), but functioned as a single unit. Business and homes served as the center of colony life.

During the fourth period, 1945 to the present, new migration has continued from Greece and the mainland U.S., and also from Australia, Africa, and elsewhere. Pioneers and new immigrants joined together in 1968 to establish an Orthodox Church that is the new center of the community. Approximately 3,000 Greeks live today on five of the eight islands and participate in all aspects of Island life even while ethnicity is reinforced and thriving.

First Period: Arrivals in a Polynesian Kingdom

Hawaiian culture developed about 2,000 years ago. Probably in the second century A.D., Polynesian navigators used their knowledge of the sun, stars, and ocean to accomplish immense

in the Revolution and Counterrevolution," *Hawaiian Journal of History,* 15 (1981), pp. 1-23; and Helen Geracimos Chapin, "The Greeks of Hawaii: An Odyssey From Kingdom to Statehood," *The Hellenic Journal,* 17 Feb., 3 Mar., and 17 Mar. 1983.

[3]The designation "Polynesian" was given to the region's inhabitants by 18th century French explorers.

voyages over unchartered ocean in open double-hulled canoes, from southern Pacific islands to the northern Hawaiian chain. The long voyages ceased about 1200 A.D., leading to the solidification of a tribal, oral, communal, and family-oriented society with a nature-based religion rich in meaning for its people.[4] Later some of these values were to blend with those from Greece. Before the arrival of non-Hawaiians in 1778, Native Hawaiians lived in an isolated equilibrium with their remarkably benign environment, free from infectious diseases, and with physical and spiritual sustenance for all.

The arrival of, first, the British under Captain James Cook, and then subsequent waves of explorers and traders from throughout the world thrust Hawaii into a turbulent international life. Various European powers—the British, French, Russians, Germans—contended with each other and with Americans for dominance. The Hawaiians, a welcoming and inclusive culture, began a 200-year struggle to maintain their identity amidst radical changes.

The Orthodox religion was carried on Russian ships as early as 1804, ahead of American missionaries from New England who brilliantly succeeded in establishing their brand of Protestantism. The Americans' arrival in 1820 produced antagonism between themselves and those unsympathetic with their aims which was to prevail into the twentieth century. When the dour Protestant missionary, Hiram Bingham, witnessed Orthodox rituals on a Russian vessel in Honolulu harbor, he remarked that he supposed one should be grateful that those of the "Greek religion" were Christians at all.[5]

Sailors from many nations reached Hawaii on trading vessels and whalers, some not to leave again, like "George Joseph a Greek, washed overboard and drowned." When an Orthodox

[4]For Hawaiian history, see: Gavan Daws, *Shoal of Time: A History of the Hawaiian Islands* (New York: Macmillan, 1968); Lawrence H. Fuchs, *Hawaii Pono: A Social History* (New York: Harcourt, Brace & World, 1961); Edward Joesting, *Hawaii: An Uncommon History* (New York: W. W. Norton, 1972); and Noel J. Kent, *Hawaii: Islands Under the Influence* (New York: Monthly Review Press, 1983).

[5]Hiram Bingham, *A Resident of Twenty-one Years in the Sandwich Islands; or the Civil, Religious and Political History of Those Islands* (Hartford, Conn.: Hezekiah Huntington, 1847), p. 151. James Michener, in his novel *Hawaii*, based the character of Abner Hale on Bingham.

funeral procession for an unfortunate sailor proceeded to the Honolulu burial yard, the local populace, egged on by the New Englanders, jeered and laughed at the chanting "idolaters."[6] It should be noted that the Americans, determined to establish their ethos, were just as hostile to Roman Catholics, Mormons, and other religious groups.

The "missionary party," as these people came to be called, was made up of the missionaries, their descendants, business allies, and associates. What was at stake was not just the question of religious "truth" but, more importantly, who was to control the economic and political destiny of the tiny island kingdom so strategically located between North America and the Far East. Greeks were to ally themselves politically, socially, and economically with other Europeans and native Hawaiians, in opposition to the Americans. Hawaiians from the mid-nineteenth century on came to prefer the more tolerant value system of Europe than rule by Puritan taboo. For example, when two young princes, both to become kings, traveled abroad in 1850, they were discriminated against in the U.S. but were treated kindly in Paris by, among others, the Greek minister to France. Hawaiians also accurately perceived that America posed the greatest threat to their own nation.

Underscoring rising American domination was the appearance in the 1840s of the United States Wilkes Exploring Expedition. Interestingly, a young Naval officer, Lieutenant George Colvocoresses, a member of that expedition, was the first Greek American to publish a book. This contained a description of the "Sandwich Islands," or Hawaii, and favorably compared the great Hawaiian King Kamehameha I to Philip of Macedon.[7]

Connections between Hawaii and Greece increased in the

[6]George Joseph, a Greek, from the *Gatherer*, as reported by the *Friend*, 2 Nov. 1875, p. 93; *Sandwich Island Gazette and Journal of Commerce*, 12 Jan. 1839. The dead sailor was taken to the Seamen's Chapel burial yard.

[7]Lieut. George M. Colvocoresses, *Four Years in a Government Exploring Expedition* . . . (New York: Cornish, Lamport & Co., 1852), pp. 187-88, said: ". . . my imagination suggested to me, that I beheld . . . one of those extraordinary natures . . . [like] Philip of Macedon . . . a man who overcame every disadvantage, and extended the narrow sovereignty of Macedon into the universal monarch of Greece, and under his son, of the then known world." Capt. Cook assigned the name "Sandwich Islands" to the archipelago in honor of his patron, the Earl of Sandwich.

first period. Not only did Colvocoresses admire the Hawaiians, but they, in turn, admired the Greeks. Partly to counteract his American advisors assumptions of Anglo-Saxon superiority, King David Kalākaua wrote in his major study on Greek mythology of the links between ancient Polynesia and Greece.[8] An educated man, he speculated that the ancestors of the modern Hawaiian race had originated in the Mediterranean region and had migrated across the southern Asian continent into the Pacific. He cited close similarities between Greek and Oceanic mythological tales of gods and goddesses, heroes and heroines. (One is struck, too, by the almost exact duplication of the crescent-shaped helmets worn by both ancient Greek and Hawaiian warriors.) The first monarch to circumnavigate the globe, in 1881, Kalakaua in Egypt danced with the handsome wife of the Greek consul. Public buildings at home adapted classical architecture, including the beautiful Iolani Palace in Honolulu. Commissioned by Kalakaua and modeled after the Athenian home of Heinrich Schleimann, excavator of Troy, it is, today, the only palace in the U.S.[9]

The Anglo-Saxons also admired Greek classical culture. Missionaries traveled from Hawaii to the Mediterranean and wrote glowingly of the Parthenon and Acropolis. Hawaiian- and English-language newspapers from their inception in 1834, in fact, carried a surprisingly large amount of material on Greece, such as travel accounts, coverage of political events, and figures on annual sugar consumption. At home in the missionary-sponsored schools, the children acted in "Greek tableaux" and studied Greek and Latin while their parents supported a library called the Atheneum. They gave the name of Tantalus to a mountain peak above Honolulu after school boys easily climbed it but had great difficulty descending.

Second Period: Greek Royalists

Missionary admiration of ancient Greece stopped short of

[8][King David] Kalakaua, *The Legends and Myths of Hawaii: The Fables and Folklore of a Strange People* (New York: Charles L. Webster, 1888), pp. 61 and 67-99.

[9]Iolani Palance served as the capitol building for the territory and the state until 1965.

extension to its modern sons. During the second period, 1880 to 1900, William D. Alexander, a missionary son, warned a church group in Honolulu in 1886 to beware of "commercial, ingenuous and eloquent, but deceitful, dirty and immoral" Greeks.[10] This warning coincided with permanent residence of Greek men in the kingdom.

In these two decades, up to 50 men entered the country and resided for at least a year. They reached Hawaii in three ways: as individual wanderers or adventurers; with recruited sugar cane workers from the Portuguese-held Azores Islands; and as kinship groups from Sparta and several villages. From one Greek settler just prior to 1860, the number increased to 12 in 1890, to 26 in 1895, dropped to 21 in 1896, and rose again, to 46 in 1900.[11]

The men were responding directly or indirectly to the rise of sugar agriculture, an industry that came to dominate Hawaiian economic and social life for a hundred years. This burgeoning capitalist industry and its attendant needs for goods and services drew people from all over the world. The native Hawaiian population could not fill labor needs. Because of centuries of isolation, it had no immunity to infectious diseases carried from the West and East. Hawaiians declined from 350,000 or more at the time of Cook's arrival, to half that number by 1820, to fewer than 30,000 by 1900. (Although "ethnic Hawaiians," that is, those with some Hawaiian blood, make up 19 percent of the present population of over 1,000,000, pure Hawaiians continue in mortal decline—there are only about 6,000 today in their native land.)[12]

[10]W. D. Alexander, "Bulgaria," in the *Friend*, August 1886, pp. 9-10. This was a paper read at the Honolulu Fort Street Church Monthly Concert of Prayer for Missions.

[11]Greeks were not counted by Hawaiian census takers. I have extracted a count from Island directories, newspapers, ships' manifests, plantation records, government documents in the Hawaii State Archives, and oral history. *The Twelfth Census of the United States Taken in the Year 1900*, vol. 1 (Washington, D.C.: United States Census Office, 1901) erroneously listed 55 Greeks because it included Galicians among them.

[12]Native Hawaiian population figures are highly political and fluctuate wildly. Estimates range from 150,000 to 900,000 at the time of Cook's arrival, the latter a figure that makes the subsequent decline of the Native population that much more horrifying. The standard sources for population statistics, which accept Cook's estimates of 300,000 to 350,000, are: Eleanor C. Nordyke, *The Peopling of Hawaii* (Honolulu: University Press of Hawaii, 1977), and Robert C. Schmitt,

The first contract laborers, Chinese, were imported in 1852. A Reciprocity Treaty, signed by the U.S. and Hawaii in 1876, by which each admitted the others' products duty-free, led to feverish economic expansion. The Hawaiian government and the sugar planters' organization cast their recruiting nets wide—from China, Japan, Korea, and the Philippines, to Portugal, Germany, Norway, Galicia, Puerto Rico, Spain, Russia, and Italy. In 95 years, 400,000 non-natives entered Hawaii.

Greek men, who were not recruited directly from Greece itself, arrived independently first in New York, then worked their way westward to Chicago and San Francisco. Ships' rosters reveal they traveled frequently and casually between Hawaii and the West Coast and even to Australia and back.

The migration of Greeks into Hawaii in this period is on a smaller scale than that into the U.S. but also is significantly different. The main migration of 1890-1910 into the U.S. was of males 18 to 35 years of age and arose from a population explosion and lack of land and work in Greece and the lure of an industrializing America.[13] Migration into Hawaii, ahead of the U.S. floodtide, arose as much from adventurousness as from poverty, and responded to Hawaii's position by the late nineteenth century as the center of Pacific trade. From the Gold Rush days of 1848 to the century's end, California served as the main market for Hawaiian exports and the main supplier of goods to the Islands.

Regarding the first group of individual wanderers, by 1879 there are records of a day laborer who was born in Greece and resided in an outlying district on the Big Island of Hawaii. After a brush with the law over disputed ownership of a horse, Nicholas Zabat, the forerunner of other "birds of passage," disappeared.

In the second group, recruited sugar workers, at least six Greek men were signed up in the Azores with Portuguese contract laborers between 1879 and 1884. When they had left

Demographic Statistics of Hawaii: 1778-1965 (Honolulu: University of Hawaii Press, 1968).

13I am indebted, of course, to Theodore Saloutos, *The Greeks in the United States* (Cambride, Mass.: Harvarad University Press, 1964). Although Saloutos did not include Hawaii's Greeks, his study is a basic source for the Greek experience.

Greece for the Azores is unknown. In Hawaii, they underwent name changes, from Dagramaticas, for example, to Karlos, then Carlos, and from Poulos to Poole. They became *lunas,* or plantation overseers, and married Portuguese or Hawaiian women. These men and their families were absorbed into the local life style although one made himself known in the 1890s to a fellow Greek, "Me like you, me Greek, not Portuguese."[14] Descendants today still retain memories of their Greek ancestry.

The men who formed the main colony originated from Sparta, the nearby villages of Vasara, Goritza, and Tsintzina, and from Arahova to the north. There were two interrelated clans or brothers, cousins, nephews, and fellow villagers—the Lycurgus-Camarinos clan and the Capilos family. John Lycurgus reached the U.S. during the American Civil War (the name in Greece was Likouros but was changed at some point in the U.S.), served in the Union army, claimed homestead land in California after the war, and was followed by kinsmen in the early 1870s. One can see in operation an informal chain migration system, the oldest having departed first from Greece, followed by younger family members and, later, by friends. All were single, between 15 and 45 years of age. Most were of peasant background and had only a few years of formal schooling.

Two factors led to their quick success. Because they usually sojourned first in the United States, they had acquired proficiency in English. In Hawaii, they quickly picked up the useful Hawaiian language. They also had had time to accumulate capital and could seize commercial opportunities. They set up wholesale produce houses in San Francisco and ranged as far as Mexico to buy fresh fruits and vegetables. By 1888, their goods filled their own refrigerators on trans-Pacific steamers. These men engaged in a lucrative triangular trade whereby they shipped fresh produce, seafood, and wines from California to Hawaii, picked up Hawaiian produce for Australia and New Zealand, and from there carried meat and butter to Hawaii, where they on-loaded fresh goods for California. From one $25 box of fruit in 1885,

[14]Difficulty in identifying Greeks among the Portuguese rests in part on the similarities of their names: Costas and Costa, for example, and Capilos and Capellos. Place of birth, however, appears in the raw data of the 1900 U.S. Census.

their exports increased by 1893 to weekly shipments of several thousand dollars each.

In the Islands, they operated various small businesses, like grocery stores, cafes, wine and liquor outlets, a rooming house, produce ranch, pineapple growing and shipping enterprise, bath house, messenger service, and a well-known hotel. They also engaged in opium smuggling. In the second half of the nineteenth century, the opium trade was carried on by the entire spectrum of Hawaii's residents. Although they easily fit into business practices of the kingdom and into the European and Hawaiian social pattern of conviviality and racial mixing, these early Greek settlers leased or rented premises and did not become Hawaiian citizens; they held to the dream of so many Greeks abroad, of going home. They lived the paradox of a craving for economic betterment that made them leave Greece and a powerful nationalism that kept them Greek.

They were known as the "Spartan colony" and were led by Peter Camarinos and George Lycurgus. Camarinos, who probably arrived in 1883 (newspaper ads promoting his California Wine Company appeared in early 1884), and Lycurgus, who arrived in 1889, were models of the pioneer trailblazer. Lycurgus's record, however, is the longest and most influential—he lived to be 101, and his years in Hawaii spanned the monarchy (to 1893), provisional government (1893-1895), republic (1895-1900), territory (1900-1959), and statehood (1959). From Vasara, he had parlayed selling lemons and candy on New York City streets to a popular San Francisco Bay area restaurant. He was like other "marginal men" scrambling for a toehold—a risk-taker filled with restless energy, a keenly developed business sense, and not overly concerned with respectability. When he arrived in Hawaii he attended the king's birthday *lûáu* (feast) and played poker with the monarch and his friends. With $4,000 from the sale of his California restaurant, he leased a Waikiki beachfront hotel. The bohemian Lycurgus, with his dashing panama hat, and his cummerbund and white suit in the style of the king, was known in his circle as the "Duke of Sparta."

The Spartans strongly held to group *ethnikos* or group belongingness. The men spoke English and Hawaiian to others but Greek among themselves. Without a church, they informally observed Orthodox holy days. They eagerly welcomed compatriot visitors—peddlers, merchants, a cigar maker, a candy maker, a flamboyant showman who entertained Honoluluans with feats of strength and magic, even a prince of Greece.[15] When one was ill, in trouble with the law, or short of money, the others rallied around him. Perhaps their most significant—certainly, their most colorful—contribution to Hawaiian history was their response to a rising Hawaiian nationalism in the 1880s and their involvement in the heated political events of the 1890s.

When the king died in 1891, his sister became queen. Two years later, on January 17, 1893, the missionary party, supported by an American gunboat in Honolulu harbor and the American minister to Hawaii, conspired in a revolution that overthrew Liliuokalani. Her crime in their eyes was that she wished to return constitutional rights to the throne and her people, rights lost in the "bayonet constitution" forced upon her brother in 1887 by so-called "reformers." After the overthrow, the prevailin *haole* (Caucasian) oligarchy formed a provisional government and bent all its efforts toward securing American annexation.

A counterrevolution was now mounted by native Hawaiians, Europeans, Canadians, and a few Americans outside the power strtucture. The Greeks rushed to the defence of the monarchy and to a man were for Hawaii remaining an independent country. Seven Greek men actively participated in the counterrevolution, and the others, like George Andreos and the Capilos brothers, were supportive behind the scenes. Plans were hatched at the Lycurgus Sans Souci Hotel, and Peter Camarinos arranged the shipment of guns, concealed in his brother Demetrios's cargoes, from the West Coast to the Islands. Several men were soldiers who fought the provisional government in the field. Within days of the uprising on January 7, 1895, the rebels were crushed by well-financed and organized government troups.[16]

The government then arrested the queen and 190 others, including five Greek men, and charged the latter with conspiracy and treason. Lycurgus and Camarinos both served jail sentences. Another significant pattern had already emerged that was dif-

[15]Greek Prince Theodore's visit to Hawaii was reported in the *Pacific Commercial Advertiser*, 4 Oct. 1901.

[16]The best source for these years is Albertine Loomis, *For Whom Are the Stars?* (Honolulu: University Press of Hawaii, 1976).

ferent from first-generation experience elsewhere—a sophisticated use of the law to defend their interests. They hired excellent legal representation by the same attorney who defended the queen, but they lost their cases and their businesses. Several accepted exile from Hawaii. Others who were not charged with crimes were nonetheless disheartened by the turn of events and returned to the mainland or to Greece.

The question of legality and illegality is informative. Law is a form of social control and defines who is deviant and who is not.[17] From 1778 to 1900 (some would argue to the present), Hawaii was subject to imposed Western law. It is an almost textbook case of a non-Western society dominated by an elite group that sought modernization and development. The entire question of legality and illegality, for example, is raised over whether Hawaii was stolen from its people in the 1893 revolution. At this time, more than a million acres of Hawaiian government lands were seized by the provisional government, then were ceded in 1898 to the U.S. These actions remain at the heart of the argument for reparations.

Use of the law for their own purposes worked well for the Greeks before the revolution. They hired clever lawyers outside the power elite. From 1883 to 1893 they initiated some 50 separate legal actions, primarily for leases, business licenses, and partnerships. From 1895 to 1898, the law worked against them, for they now had to defend themselves against charges of criminal activities.

As to the overthrow of the monarchy, President Cleveland wanted to wash his hands of the whole dirty business, and the bill for annexation at first could not clear the U.S. Congress. But history decreed Hawaii would become part of America. The location of a deep natural harbor at Pearl Harbor and events in the Philippines during the Spanish-American War of 1898 thrust the Islands' military importance into prominence.

At the century's end, with the necessity to enlarge harbor facilities and meet the needs of a growing city, about a dozen Greek men were hired on the West Coast for dock construction and sewer projects in Honolulu. They worked out their two-year contracts, then returned to California. In New York, eleven Greek men were recruited for the sugar plantations. They broke their contracts within ten days after arrival and made newspaper headlines by charging they were lied to by the sugar planters' agents about wages and living conditions.

Third Period: Permanence and Family Life

Several distinct settlement patterns in work and family lives emerged in the third period, 1900 to 1941. After Hawaii became a territory in 1900, the general aim for those who remained and for those who now arrived was permanence. The events of the 1890s had taken their toll, with the tragic early deaths of the Camarinos brothers and the harassment of others by Republic of Hawaii officials who either denied them business licenses or annoyed them by filing criminal charges against them at their business locations, usually for "illegal sales of alcohol" and for "disorderly conduct."

The geographic isolation of Hawaii and its peculiar historical development affected settlement. The Caucasian elite that had fought for racial, economic, social, and political superiority in the nineteenth century became the oligarchy that cemented its power in the twentieth century. This oligarchy, which ran Hawaii as a feudal plantation stronghold, consigned the darker-skinned races, except for *alii* (nobility or upper class) Hawaiians, to secondary status. But economically Hawaii now required a middle class. Thus the "lesser haoles"—Lawrence Fuch's phrase[18]—who were small businessmen, school teachers, minor officials, and the like, were expected to emulate the oligarchy's conservative republican values and identify with them.

Migration after 1900 from Europe widened to include Greeks who now traveled directly to Hawaii, only a few sojourning first on the mainland. New migrants came from Milos, Kalymnos, Pyrgos, Samos, Rhodes, Crete, and Constantinople. Regardless of their places of origin, they only partly bought into these conservative values, retaining their sense of distinctiveness from other Caucasians. American citizenship in 1900 was automatically con-

[17]Harry Miller Blickhahn, *Uncle George of Kilauea: The Story of George Lycurgus* (Hawaii National Park: Volcano House, 1961) is the authorized, privately printed version of his life.

ferred on citizens of Hawaii, which the Greeks were not. Nor did they rush forward now to be naturalized. They remained Hawaiian royalists in spirit and influenced incoming compatriots in this regard, and at the same time they capitalized on their own talents. George Lycurgus turned his earlier notoriety into positive action when he reestablished his businesses and formed the "Jailbirds of 1895." The "Jailbirds" met yearly at his restaurant on the anniversary of the counterrevolution. Lycurgus and his nephews and cousins also regularly observed the queen's birthday until her death in 1916. New immigrants and the families they acquired, who had never known Hawaiian royalty, sentimentally called Kalakaua and Liliuoklani "the King" and "the Queen."

America's entrance into World War I partly appealed to their patriotism. Before the war, in 1912, a half dozen had paid their own passages back to Greece to fight in the Balkan Wars. Several then returned to serve in the American army in 1917-1918. Most seemed, however, to have developed dual primary loyalties to Hawaii and Greece. By 1920 only 15 percent were citizens. Restrictive immigration laws of the 1920s and the desire to import wives led to naturalization of 50 percent by 1930.

Compared to mainland Greeks and in response to the growing American commercial and military presence in the territory, they enjoyed great job diversity. They were bartenders, café owners, cooks, policemen, farmers, cowboys, candy makers, soldiers and sailors, engineers, jewelers, proprietors of military cafés, and fishermen. There was a railroad switchman, an orchestra conductor, a professor, and a professional wrestler. In one person, George Lycurgus, we find a hotel proprietor (the Hilo Hotel and Volcano House), restaurant owner (the Union Café and Demosthenes Café, the latter with his nephew) a lumber mill and jewelry store partner (the Pahoa Lumber Mill and Detor's Jewelers, the latter with John Detor and George Michopulos), and real estate developer. As he had in the 1890s, after 1900 he led the way in sponsoring the importation of relatives and compatriots to work in his many enterprises until they could strike out on their own. Called "Barba Yorgos" by them, he came to be known Island-wide as "Uncle George" and his hotel in the Hawaii National Park, the Volcano House, as "Uncle George's hotel."[19]

Arranging for family lives was more of a problem than establishing work lives. One group of men, undoubtedly lonely and unwilling or unable to spend the travel time and money it took to arrange Greek marriages, formed unions with Hawaiian, Portuguese, and German women. A smaller group of males held to their desire for Greek wives. After securing their own livelihoods, they traveled the long voyage back to Greece or to American cities like Boston and San Francisco to find women. Once again George Lycurgus led the way. In 1903, he brought Athena Geracimos Lycurgus from Sparta, and the first all-Greek child was born to them in Hawaii in 1904. Athena and George Lycurgus together were responsible directly or indirectly for 11 of the 12 women who settled in Hawaii between 1903 and 1941. Families thus established formed the core of the permanent colony, and their descendants are still leaders in today's cultural life. All the Greek women but one were of a higher social class than their husbands. They were from middle class backgrounds but without prospects. They chose both a practical and adventurous route for themselves, to leave families and familiar surroundings and accompany the men across thousands of miles to a strange and unknown place. Filled with life and vitality, they became best friends among themselves, exchanged child-keeping responsibilities, and in other ways fostered a community. One small enclave near downtown Honolulu consisted of three homes, five extended families, and single male boarders. A second-generation daughter recalls wryly but affectionately that it was like having five mothers disciplining her.

The homes and downtown businesses served together as a community center. Colony members exchanged newspapers from the mainland and read letters from "home" to each other. Because there was no Church, there was no Greek school. The women as culture carriers took up the task of passing on language maintenance and customs. The most devout set up home altars. Because there was no "Greektown," however, the men and women mingled with non-Greeks to a far greater degree

---

[18]See Helen Geracimos Chapin, "From Sparta to Spencer Street: Greek Women in Hawaii," *Hawaiian Journal of History*, 13 (1979): pp. 136-156.

than their mainland counterparts. Inevitability, outside forces
entered the colony. Greek children attended local schools, the
boys taking up football, the girls hula dancing. The Hawaiian
spirit of welcoming strangers and being inclusive rather than
exclusive has influenced all immigrants into Hawaii over two
centuries.

In such a small, close-knit community of about 200, second-
generation children of marriageable age presented a difficulty.
The children felt like brothers and sisters to each other. Several
families went to great expense and trouble to arrange Greek
marriages for their daughters and nieces, but inevitably outmar-
riages occurred to other Caucasians and Hawaiians. When
grandchildren arrived, the first generation's tolerance increased
even more.

More than 50 percent of the pioneer men who married, or
about 18 out of 30, did so to non-Greek women. Mixed families formed by these unions had their own dynamics. Generally
these families did not remain in the colony, although there was
continuing contact over the years. The degree of contact seemed
to depend on whether the kinsmen stayed in business with each
other and whether the wives were compatible. A majority of
the wives of mixed unions worked outside the home. Fully one
half of the marriages ended in divorce. By the end of the 1980s
only a few descendants of these pioneer mixed marriages had
kept ties to the community.

By comparison, in the all-Greek families only one wife
worked outside the home, and she represented the only divorce
in the group. Other wives helped in the family businesses but
did not consider this "work." The descendants from pioneer all-
Greek couples maintain strong community ties even though they
themselves have entered mixed marriages. Interestingly, second-
and third-generation members have adopted non-Greek children,
following the Hawaiian custom of *hanai* (adoption) that is
based on the belief that every child should have a family.

At least 40 men in this period remained single. Some were
marginal all their lives, like the solitary railroad switchman who
came to town on Saturdays. Known to colony members only as
"Mr. Saturday," he left $200,000 to relatives in Greece after his
death. Others interacted regularly with the families, even board-

ing in their homes and attending the large gatherings at Sunday beach picnics.

In Hawaii, there was less factionalism than on the mainland. While jealousies and falling-outs occurred, colony members rallied on the occasion of a wedding, funeral, or birthday. During the Depression there was only one bankruptcy—those in financial trouble were helped out by the better-off until they could recover. Although Demetrios Camarinos had established a benevolent society in California before 1900, in Hawaii there were none, nor were there regional societies. Men and women joined such diverse groups as the Masonic orders, Shriners, and beach clubs. Non-Greeks who spoke Greek, like a small group of Jewish males from Smyrna, formed friendly social alliances with the colony. There was little division by Greek politics, like Venizelists and Royalists. Hawaiian politics again engaged the settlers' interest. In an era when it was almost subversive not to be a Republican, those who became citizens and voted did so for Democrats. Many recalled discrimination in mainland cities before they moved to Hawaii, and they sympathized with the local struggles of an underdog labor class against the power elite.

Fourth Period: Assimilation and Ethnic Renewal

World War II was another great catalyst of change in Hawaii. Island Greeks, like their mainland counterparts, were cut off from family and friends in Greece for the duration of the War. Patriotism now more clearly encompassed loyalty to Greece and America. Islanders led Greek War Relief projects and U.S. war bond drives and opened their homes to military personnel.

From the war's end to 1965, new immigration and settlement occurred in two ways. Pioneers hastened to sponsor relatives suffering from the German occupation and the Civil War. In addition, Greeks unconnected to Islanders entered from Europe, as well as second- and third-generation men and women from mainland cities, Australia, New Zealand, Africa, and elsewhere.

Postwar years brought further important changes. The 1950s witnessed a Democratic revolution that broadened the power base to include Japanese Americans, Hawaiians, and the "lesser haoles." Statehood in 1959 ushered in enormous growth and development. Depending on one's viewpoint, Hawaii is still a distant magnet—today it boasts or suffers one of the highest per capita immigration ratios of all the states. It now has a service economy, for tourism and defense are the two main industries.

From the end of World War II to the end of the 1980s there has been a steady broadening of participation and thus greater assimilation in the general life of the state by resident Greeks. Conversely, they are more visible than ever. On the one hand, Greeks are dispersed throughout the major islands and are employed in the private and public sectors as doctors, lawyers, engineers, nurses, dentists, teachers, athletes, government officials, architects, social workers, bankers, real estate brokers, military personnel, and broadcast journalists. The old family-owned businesses with low ethnic profiles, like the Merchant's Grill and the Monte Carlo Café, are gone. On the other hand, enterprises like "It's Greek to Me," the "Greek Taverna," and "Athenian Dimitri's Greek Facials," capitalize on ethnicity, which is good business.

Ethnicity also can be good politics. The 1983 centennial celebration of Greeks in Hawaii was officially opened by the Japanese-American governor and his wife. The present governor, a native Hawaiian, the Honolulu mayor, of Italian American ancestry, and their Japanese American wives attend the yearly Greek festival, as do other public officials like state legislators.

Yet there are only 3,000 Greeks in Hawaii, and about 20 percent of these are in the mobile military population. How does one account for their influence? There is no doubt that Greeks have benefited from the rise of ethnic consciousness in general. In addition, while mingling in the greater community, they have retained cohesiveness. To a surprising degree, one still hears the language spoken. Islanders visit their relatives in Greece or on the mainland and are in turn visited by them. Island Greeks, as they have for a hundred years, still strongly identify with Hawaii and take pride in being distnctive from the larger *haole* population.

There is another important reason why ethnic identity has prevailed amid multiculturalism. The single most nurturing factor is undoubtedly the establishment in 1968 of an Orthodox Church which itself promotes Greekness and cosmopolitanism. Orthodoxy historically has been nationalistic but not exclusively racial, which makes it comfortable in the Hawaiian environment. Having come late to Hawaii—the smallness of the pre-World War II community could not support a church—Saints Constantine and Helen Greek Orthodox Church has rushed to catch up to its unique role. It is known also as the Eastern Orthodox Church, an indication of its appeal to all Orthodox throughout the State. On any Sunday the Church altar and icons are decked in flower *leis*. Services are held regularly in Greek, English, and Slovenian, and on special holy days also in Russian, French, German, Japanese, and Hawaiian—or many of the groups represented in the congregation. The Women's Philoptochos Society "Aloha Chapter" engages in good works in the greater community. Each priest from the mainland has encouraged inclusion of Hawaiian history in the yearly festival the Church sponsors, the Church thus celebrating its Greek and Hawaiian roots. The festival is held at a public beach park and draws 15,000.

The need for community is a powerful human drive. Every group is a minority in contemporary Hawaii: Caucasians represent only 25 percent of the population. Interdependence is a daily necessity. Cultural identity is not an either/or proposition. The Greeks in Hawaii, as in the past, have been influenced by the Hawaiian spirit of *aloha* and have, in turn, contributed to and enriched that spirit. They have constructed for themselves a meaningful combination of values and have found ethnic strength in a society of many cultures.

Crisis in the Family: Padrones and Radicals in Utah, 1908-1912[1]

GUNTHER W. PECK

During the brief, but severe economic depression of 1908, nine Greek laborers from Bingham, Utah, wrote a letter to the editor of the local Greek newspaper, *Ergatis* ("Worker") praising the Greek padrone Leonidas Skliris for finding them jobs:

> We consider it our duty to express in public our deepest thanks to our great protector, Leonidas Skliris, who is never tired, ever energtic, and always successful in defending the laborer in his every care and need.[2]

Just four years later, however, eight hundred Greek workers dug trenches, stockpiled ammunition, and stole dynamite in an impassioned attempt to eliminate the labor contracting system in Bingham. Greek strikers were joined by hundreds of Italian and Japanese miners with similar grievances against their padrones. What accounts for this explosive transformation? What was the precise nature of the padrone-worker relationship in 1908 and why did it change so dramatically over the next four years? How ideologically radical had immigrant workers become and

[1]This essay is adapted from chapters three and four of my master's thesis, "Ethnicity and Labor Radicalism in the West: Immigrants and Padrones in Utah, 1908-1912," University of Wisconsin-Madison, 1989. I am greatly indebted to Helen Papanikolas, whose pathbreaking work sparked my initial interest in padronism.

[2]*Ergatis*, 8/1/08, p. 3. *Ergatis* was printed in Katharevousa Greek and was published weekly in Salt Lake City, Utah, between September 1907, and October 1908. Assistance in translating these recently discovered sources was provided by Ms. Lena Nikolaou of Thessaloniki, Greece.

what was their relationship to their union, the Western Federation of Miners? Put simply, what did unionism mean to Greek and other immigrant strikers in the fall of 1912?

These questions each address in different ways the historic relationship between class and ethnicity among immigrant workers. The complexities of this relationship have unfortunately been obscured by specialization within the historical literature. Greek immigration historian Helen Papanikolas has brilliantly illuminated the vital importance of ethnic culture in the Bingham strike, but strenuously avoided ascribing any aspects of Greek behavior to class consciousness.[3] By contrast, Greek labor historian Dan Georgakas has recently argued that the Greek strikers in Bingham were class conscious and not simply motivated by the sense of Greek *philotimo* or "love of honor."[4] Confronted with the theoretical choice between class and ethnicity, Papanikolas chose ethnicity while Georgakas chose class as the independent variables determining Greek workers' behavior and ideology.[5]

Class and ethnicity are not antithetical or mutually exclusive historical forces, however, but often closely related aspects of immigrant workers' experience. Class consciousness among Greek workers in Bingham was not the product of some objective economic calculus, but grew out of their dynamic social relationships with both padrones and employers, relationships in which culture—Greek and American—exerted profound influence.[6] Ethnicity was not a static constellation of old world rituals, nor a cross-class consciousness, but a dynamic cultural identity that included class arrangements which could both nurture and undercut labor militancy. The relationship between class and ethnicity represented no linear tradeoff, but was highly complex and permeated nearly every aspect of life in Bingham, from political

    [3]See Helen Papanikolas, "Toil and Rage in a New Land: The Greek Immigrants in Utah," *Utah Historical Quarterly*, 38:2 (Spring 1970), 100-204.
    [4]See Dan Georgakas, "The Greeks in America," *Journal of the Hellenic Diaspora*, 14 (Spring-Summer 1987), pp. 5-62.
    [5]For a recent attempt to bridge this artificial juxtaposition between labor and immigration history, see Dirk Hoerder's collection of essays entitled *"Struggle a Hard Battle": Essays on Working-Class Immigrants* (Dekalb, Illinois: Northern Illinois Press, 1986).
    [6]This flexible understanding of class consciousness owes much to Sean Wilentz's discussion of class formation in his recent study, *Chants Democratic: New York City and the Rise of the American Working Class, 1788-1850* (New York: Oxford University Press, 1985), pp. 10-13.

efforts to curb alcohol consumption to "rowdiness" in Bingham's coffeehouses and saloons.

The Padrone-Worker Relationship

The relationship between padrones and immigrant workers was reciprocal—the padrone provided jobs and a measure of job security while workers paid him their tribute, usually $20 for the job and a dollar a month to keep it. Power was not equal in this relationship nor were the terms of employment freely negotiated, but padrones relied upon the formal consent of immigrant workers. Greek workers, for example, signed a pseudo-legal contract which authorized Leonidas Skliris to take his monthly pay cut from their wages. While nothing in these contracts bound the actions of Skliris and other padrones, unspoken codes of honor and obligation nonetheless governed their conduct. If the padrone overstepped what workers believed were mutually prescribed limits to his authority, workers reacted violently.[7]

In 1908, the ties of social dependency between the Greek padrone and newly-arrived Greek workers fueled both familial harmony and explosive anger. Even as some Greek workers were praising Skliris as their "great protector," other Greek padrones were coming under sharp attack. *Ergatis* editor Panayiotis Siouris denounced a Greek interpreter in Bingham, one Dimitris Brousalis, for "exploiting the poor laborer" by charging them "twenty to fifty dollars in order to get a job." Siouris's editorial described Brousalis as a "creature, not Greek, not even human" and called upon laborers to send in any information regarding similar "profiteering." Siouris received a flood of responses, most of which described their padrones as traitors to Greece or, worse, as Turks. A Greek trackman in Pocatello, Idaho, for example, compared his padrone, William Caravelis, to Greece's foreign enemies in the Balkans: "What more do the Bulgars do

[7]For a more detailed analysis of reciprocal class relationships in which power is negotiated between dominant and subordinate parties, see Eugene Genovese's classic work, *Roll, Jordan, Roll: The World the Slaves Made* (New York: Pantheon Books, 1974). A copy of one of Skliris's contracts survives in the Greek archives of the University of Utah's Marriott Library.

in Macedonia?" Another Pocatello worker described Caravelis as the "Ali-Pasha of Pocatello," and called on his "dear compatriots" to "continue your holy task" of speaking out against the padrone.[8] These letters reflected Greek workers' sense of patriotism and *philotimo*, but they also revealed the narrow limits to Greek workers' militancy in 1908. The anger of most letters was personal, ethnic in expression, and directed toward the particular abuses of particular padrones, rather than the actual practice of labor contracting itself. These Greek workers made an implicit distinction between good and bad padrones and consequently affirmed the legitimacy of the padrone system. Siouris captured this ideological distinction well when he urged his compatriots to reject only those padrones who "dare to violate certain limits to the disadvantage of the poor laborers."[9]

Greeks and the Immigrant Working Class

Immigrant workers' perceptions of the proper "limits" to the padrone's authority were not static. They were shaped by the industrial context in which immigrant laborers lived and worked. The vast majority of Greek, Japanese, and Italian immigrants in Bingham were imported there to perform the unskilled and semiskilled jobs that the Utah Copper Company's massive technological innovations required. In 1907, the Utah Copper Company began mining low-grade copper ore with steam shovels in one of the first open-pit mining operations in the country. The radically new mining process required large amounts of unskilled immigrant labor to lay railroad tracks for the cumbersome steam shovels and to load and unload the crushed ore at the mine and smelter.[10] The resulting occupational stratification along ethnic lines is clearly visible in a comparison of the skill levels of Bingham's ethnic groups in 1910 (see Table One).

---

[8]*Ergatis*, 2/29/08, p. 1,2; *Ergatis*, 3/7/08, p. 1,5; *Ergatis*, 3/14/08, p. 3.
[9]*Ergatis*, 3/7/08, p. 1; *Ergatis*, 3/14/08, p. 1.
[10]See Leonard J. Arrington, *The Richest Hole on Earth: A History of the Bingham Copper Mine* (Logan: Utah State University Press, 1963), 90ff, and Harold Barger & Sam Schurr, *The Mining Industries 1899-1939: A Study of Output, Employment, and Productivity* (New York: Arno Press, 1972), pp. 109ff.

TABLE ONE: ETHNIC GROUPS IN BINGHAM, 1910

Ethnic	% Tot	% Unskd	% Smskd	% Skd	% Prof	% Eng	% Brd	% Part	% Male	% TimeUS
Japanese	7	100	0	0	0	0	100	4	100	4.0
Greek	23	73	20	2	5	9	87	86	100	3.5
Italian	14	25	73	0	2	31	75	52	100	4.0
Finnish	8	7	83	3	7	86	75	3	90	8.8
English	10	19	44	26	11	100	53	8	86	15.4
American	32	21	31	30	18	100	53	4	90	31.4
Total	100	35	40	15	10	62	70	30	95	15.2

"Unskd"=Unskilled; "Smskd"=Semiskilled; "Skd"=Skilled; "Prof"=Professional; "Eng"=Speaks English; "Brd"=Boarding; "Part"=Holds residential lease or deed in partnership; "TimeUS"=Time spent in the United States.

*These figures are compiled from a random one-in-ten sampling of all occupation holders in the Thirteenth Federal Census of 1910 for Bingham Canyon.

Unskilled Greek and Japanese workers received the lowest wages in Bingham—$1.75 a day, compared to $3.50 a day for skilled American workers—but it was the dangerous nature of industrial work that posed the most difficult adjustment for Bingham's immigrants. Immigrant laborers were frequently injured or killed on the job and only rarely received any compensation from the Utah Copper Company.[11] Industrial accidents provoked angry cries against American companies in Utah's immigrant communities. When two Greek cousins were killed at the Bingham smelter in 1908, the editor of the *Ergatis* cursed the smelter itself: "May thunder and fire fall upon the smelter, which has poured poison into the glasses of many parents." Other immigrants expressed their frustration with industrial work more directly in acts of industrial sabotage. In the spring of 1908, for example, two trackmen from Crete twisted several

[11]Greeks frequently sued the Utah Copper Company for compensation, despite the fact that few of them could speak English or even write. When George Kanelakis sued the Utah Copper Company to pay a compensation to the family of his brother who was killed in a rockslide on his way home from work, the company successfully defended itself in court by arguing that "the deceased well knew . . . the risks and hazards . . . (of) his employment and thereby assumed whatever risks and dangers there were." [Third District Judicial Court, Salt Lake County, Case #14286, 8/25/11, State Archives, Salt Lake City, Utah.]

train rails and subsequently destroyed three train cars. Appearing as a case of "malicious mischief" in the Bingham police records, such acts of physical sabotage were increasingly common between 1907 and 1912.[12]

The frustrations and anger produced by the immigrants' adjustment to industrial work fueled collective forms of protest and behavior. On June 23, 1908, five Greek laborers threatened to kill their American supervisor after he arbitrarily fired a member of their Greek work gang. When the supervisor tried to fire the five "impertinent" Greeks, they "started beating him with sticks" until nearby workers broke up the scuffle. Such rumblings of discontent became better organized two months later when over three hundred Greek workers walked off their jobs at the Utah Copper Company demanding a restoration of a pay cut that had taken place a month earlier. When the Utah Copper Company granted their request a few days later, the editor of *Ergatis* was astonished: "Three hundred Greeks without supervision, without being united in association, agreed upon everything. This is something we would not have believed unless we had seen it." The solidarity that Greek laborers demonstrated was unprecedented in Bingham and underscored the growing level of class consciousness, organization, and militancy among allegedly "unorganized" Greek workers.[13]

The consciousness of immigrant workers was not only shaped by work, however, but was also rooted within their experiences off the job. The great majority of Bingham Greeks, Italians, and Japanese lived in makeshift boarding houses, built out of whatever materials they might scavenge, steal, or buy, money permitting. A writer for the New York daily *Call* described Bingham's immigrant boarding houses in the following manner:

> These ill smelling places are not fit to house a dog, let alone so many human beings. . . . Dark, windowless, floorless, they are constructed out of powder boxes, the sheet

[12]*Ergatis*, 10/10/08, p. 2; *Ergatis*, 3/28/08, p. 5; Bingham Canyon Police Records, March 1909, State Archives, Salt Lake City, Utah.

[13]*Ergatis*, 7/4/08, p. 3, and Salt Lake *Tribune*, 6/24/08, p. 9; *Ergatis*, 8/22/08, p. 1, 5.

metal of tin cans and such odds and ends that the miserable builders are able to pick up without getting arrested.

The poor living conditions of Bingham's unskilled immigrant community provoked comment not merely in the national Socialist press, but also in local publications. In the fall of 1912, the normally cautious *Engineering and Mining Journal* of Salt Lake City described Bingham's residential section as a "sewer four miles long."[14]

Amidst this poverty, Greek and other immigrant workers developed a mutualistic culture, based upon common ties of ethnicity, occupation, and gender. In their boarding houses, Greek workers took turns cooking, washing, and cleaning. Greek miner Angelo Georgedes recalled his living arrangements in a board-inghouse as a young miner:

> Greek fellows working in the mines . . . probably 8, 12, 15 of them would live together. And they would take turns, some to clean the house and some to cook . . . . One day one would fix the breakfast (or) fix lunches the night before. . . . See, they didn't have no cook.

In addition to sharing domestic chores, the vast majority of Greek workers held their residential leases in partnership, thereby minimizing the financial responsibilities of any single immigrant (see Table One). Greek workers were not "individualistic" and "innately conservative" as some Greek immigration historians have contended, but fundamentally mutualistic in the ways that they adapted to industrial life in Bingham. Greek workers remained committed to their nuclear families back in Greece, but their domestic arrangements were vitally important in establishing social networks based upon their shared industrial experience in Bingham.[15]

[14]New York *Call*, 10/6/12, p. 3; *Engineering and Mining Journal*, 10/12/12, p. 676.

[15]*Reminiscences of Life and Moving to America*, Salt Lake City, Utah Historical Society, 1976; an oral history of Mr. Angelo Georgedes, interviewed by Adam Kent Powell, 12/10/76, p. 4; Zeese Papanikolas, *Buried Unsung: Louis Tikas and the Ludlow Massacre* (Salt Lake City, University of Utah Press, 1982). See pages 287-89 for his discussion of Greek workers' ideology in the West.

The ethnic saloon was the center of this all-male, working-class culture. Like Bingham's Italian and Japanese immigrants, Greeks patronized their own social and drinking establishments, where they spent much of their free time. Both secular and religious Greek traditions flourished in Bingham's coffeehouses. Visiting Greek Orthodox priests conducted liturgies in the coffeehouse and their religious articles were kept behind the bar. Traveling Greek minstrels frequently performed the Karaghiozi," or puppet of the supposedly crafty Turk." Yet, the always got the better of the supposedly crafty Turk." Yet, the coffeehouse was not merely a place which "drew minds away from America and back toward nostalgic memories of the old country," as Charles Moskos has argued. Greek workers also discussed mine conditions and their many job grievances in the coffeehouse, much as Bingham's American miners did in the local Western Federation of Miner's union hall. The coffeehouse existed at the heart of Greek workers' cultural life, a culture that was both Greek and working class.[16]

Thus, Bingham's ethnic saloons did not merely reinforce particular immigrant group identities, but also nurtured a male, working-class identity that had the potential to transcend strict ethnic lines. In all of Bingham's ethnic saloons, gambling, drinking, fighting, and prostitution were the principal forms of entertainment. Violence was an integral part of this male, working-class world. An examination of the number of civil disturbances in Bingham between 1908 and 1915 reveals a dramatic upsurge in the number of social disturbances accompanying the arrival of unskilled ethnics after 1907.[17] More than mere rowdiness or nativism, the increase in social unrest was the product of Bingham's violent working-class culture in which male honor and its defense shaped and defined expressions of social violence. Saloon fights, for example, typically originated with an insult

[16]Helen Papanikolas, "Toil and Rage," p. 118-119; Charles Moskos, "Georgakas on Greek Americans: A Response," *Journal of the Hellenic Diaspora*, 14 (Spring-Summer 1987), p. 59.

[17]Between 1908 and 1912 the number of civil disturbances skyrocketed 230 percent, far outpacing the community's more modest population increase of about 30%. The number of assault and battery cases tripled, while the number of "carrying concealed weapons" charges increased twenty-one fold. (These statistics were compiled from the Bingham police record, State Archives, Salt Lake City, Utah.)

to a miner's honor, and very often became spectator affairs that involved more than the individual participants. Some of the most celebrated social events in Bingham were the frequent wrestling matches between Japanese and Greek miners, at which hundreds of their countrymen cheered, jeered, and placed bets on the likely winner. Such fights socialized the most disparate of Bingham's ethnic groups and reflected the violent ways in which working-class culture transcended and broke down certain ethnic and racial boundaries.[18]

Crisis in the Family

Greek workers' shared experience with other unskilled immigrants in Bingham fueled a growing disillusionment with the entire padrone system. The first glimmerings of a more fundamental critique of the padrone's authority were visible in 1908 among the letters sent to the *Ergatis* protesting Caravelis's abuses. In April 1908, one Greek worker called on his fellow workers to "crush these tramps who suck our sweat," while another addressed his letter to his "brother laborers." Two months later a number of Greek workers in Bingham began fighting each other "with guns, knives, sticks, and picks" over whether tributes should be paid to the Greek padrone. No one was hurt in a shootout between "loyal" and "disloyal" Greek workers, but resentment against the padrone system soon resulted in bloodshed in the nearby coal mining town of Winter's Quarters, Utah. On June 24, 1908, Greek miner Steve Flemetis shot and killed George Demetrakopoulos, Skliris's labor contracting lieutenant for the Utah Fuel Company. According to friends of Flemetis, the murder was prompted by Demetrakopoulos's unwarranted dismissal of Flemetis from his job in the coal mine. Flemetis was never apprehended by the police and apparently escaped to his

[18]New York *Call*, 10/6/12, p. 3, and Helen Papanikolas, "Toil and Rage," p. 122; interview with Greek immigrant Jack Tallas, 1/18/71, by Theodore Paulos, Greek Oral History Collections, Marriott Library, University of Utah; *Ergatis*, 7/4/08, p. 3, and Salt Lake *Tribune*, 6/24/08, p. 9; the argument of this paragraph has been influenced by Elliott Gorn's article, "Homicide, Nativism, and Working-Class Culture in Antebellum New York City," *Journal of American History*, 74 (September, 1987), pp. 388-410.

native Crete with the help of friends in Winter's Quarters.[19]

The growing militancy and resentment of Greek laborers sent shock waves through Utah's elite Greek community. Comprised principally of merchants and a few professionals who were able to speak English, this group assumed the forms of leadership in Utah's Greek community.[20] As divisions between Greek workers and the padrone appeared to be getting out of control during the summer of 1908, editor Siouris attempted to reconcile the rifts that he had initially opened by pleading for ethnic unity:

> The Greek community of Utah since it was founded never had any parties. The word division is not in its dictionary. The Greeks move as one body, they think as one mind, they act as one head.

The chorus of angry voices and violence in the Greek community belied Siouris's attempt to evoke an image of social harmony, however. Siouris himself became increasingly critical of the rebellious actions of his working-class countrymen. When five Greek "rowdies" attacked their American supervisor on June 24, 1908, Siouris exhorted Greek workers to "be smart, be reasonable. Realize that only with discipline can you have a stable job. Don't be brave young men because here it doesn't work." In pleading with workers to exhibit more *philotimo,* Siouris highlighted the emerging differences between workers and "respectable" Greeks' understanding of ethnic honor and ironically underscored the growth of class conflict within the Greek community.[21]

Leonidas Skliris fully recognized how dangerous these developments were to his authority and consequently sought to influence the content of the *Ergatis.* After Skliris's interpreter, Deme-

[19]*Ergatis,* 3/7/08, p. 1; *Ergatis,* 5/12/08, p. 5; Salt Lake *Tribune,* 6/17/08, p. 9, and Deseret *Evening News,* 6/20/08, p. 3; Salt Lake *Tribune,* 6/24/08, p. 1.

[20]A comparison of unskilled and professional Greek immigrants in Bingham and Salt Lake City illustrates important differences between these groups; Utah's elite Greeks were much more likely to speak English, to live with family members, to have dependents, and much less likely to hold property or leases in partnership.

[21]*Ergatis,* 5/12/08, p. 1; *Ergatis,* 7/4/08, p. 1.

trakopoulos, was killed in June, the tone of the *Ergatis* abruptly changed. Throughout the summer, Siouris featured editorials which not only criticized the rebellious behavior of Greek workers but praised the benevolence of "our great protector" Leonidas Skliris. Siouris's conservative shift alienated a growing number of Greek workers and subscriptions to the *Ergatis* plummeted between May and September 1908. Skliris's concern that the faltering newspaper might be used against him should it fall into the wrong hands led him to take direct steps to control its publication. The *Ergatis* stopped publication on October 17, 1908, in large measure because Skliris had put additional financial pressure upon Siouris to close the business. Two months later, Skliris acquired the newspaper in receivership.[22]

Hostility toward Skliris and the padrone system continued to grow, however, as Greek workers became more acculturated to Bingham's immigrant working class. In February 1911, over fifty Greek laborers wrote a letter to the governor of Utah, William Spry, demanding an investigation into Skliris's tribute system.

Do you think this is right for him [Skliris] to sell livelihoods[sic] to the poor workman ... and to thus suck the blood of the poor laborer? Where are we? In the free country of Amerika[sic] or in a country dominated by a despotic form of government? ... Let us be independent in this independent country ... Hoping you will liberat [sic] us from this padrone, who is ravaging the blood of the poor laborer, and that too, of his own countrymen.

Greek workers experienced more than a sense of betrayal in 1911; they had gained a perception of their American rights and a working-class identity which challenged the very legitimacy of the padrone system. Their sense of *philotimo* was still Greek, but they had now incorporated aspects of their working-class experience in Bingham. Skliris was not merely a traitor or a Turk,

[22]*Ergatis*, 8/1/08, p. 3; *Ergatis*, 10/17/08, p. 1; Third District Judicial Court Records, Salt Lake County, Utah: Case # 11090, 3/2/09, State Archives, Salt Lake City, Utah.

but an oppressor of "the poor laborer" who had also betrayed "his own countrymen."[23]

If Skliris knew of the letter to the governor, he did not let it slow his plans to acquire greater economic control over his laboring compatriots in Bingham. Just three days after Greek workmen wrote their impassioned letter to Governor Spry, Leonidas Skliris's brother, Evangelos, acquired control of the Panhellenic grocery store in Bingham and promptly transformed it into another form of tribute for himself and his brother by requiring all Greek laborers to trade there or risk losing their jobs at the Utah Copper Company. Such machinations galvanized Greek workers' militancy, and in August of 1911 Greek workers sent another letter to Governor Spry, this one typewritten and signed by over five hundred Greek workers. The letter demanded the complete and immediate abolition of the padrone system. Spry promptly responded, but suggested that Greek workers "lay their charges before the officers of the Utah Copper Company, whom I know will accord a respectful and impartial hearing." Most immigrant workers recognized that the Utah Copper management was hardly impartial, however, and began searching for more militant and radical means of freeing themselves from "protectors" such as Leonidas Skliris and a complicit Utah Copper management.[24]

The Western Federation of Miners and the 1912 Strike

When John Lowney, organizer for the radical Western Federation of Miners, arrived in Bingham in the spring of 1912, he had little inkling that Bingham's immigrant workers were already well organized. Lowney's success in getting Bingham's immigrants to join the union was spectacular: the union grew from 250 mem-

[23]An unsigned letter from fifty Greek laborers to Governor William S. Spry, dated February 12, 1911. William S. Spry Papers, Personal Correspondence, Box 10, File "G," State Archives, Salt Lake City, Utah.

[24]Papers of the Panhellenic Grocery Company, Bingham Microfiche File #1: Bill of Sale, 2/15/11; Register of Actions, Town of Bingham, "Panhellenic Grocery vrs. John Manousakis," 1/3/12; Correspondence between Mike Lakis et al. and Governor William S. Spry, 8/10/11 & 8/17/11, William S. Spry Papers, Personal Correspondence, Box 10, File "G"; All located in State Archives, Salt Lake City, Utah.

bers in June, to 700 in July, to nearly 1200 by September. Most new members were Greeks and Italians, groups whom the WFM had targeted by hiring Italian organizer Steve Oberto and by translating the WFM's constitution and its organizing literature into Greek in June 1912. Although most Greek workers had little previous exposure to Marxist doctrine, they had little difficulty understanding the WFM's claim that the capitalist was the true foreigner when many had long considered Skliris to be a "Turk" himself. Whether or not Greek immigrants believed the rhetoric of the WFM's organizing literature, they understood the reality of class struggle, particularly within the padrone-worker relationship. A call for the abolition of the padrone system was, not surprisingly, the WFM's most effective tactic for organizing Bingham's Italian and Greek workers. In May, the WFM's local secretary, Ed Locke, wrote a letter to the Turkish ambassador in Washington demanding an investigation into Skliris's exploitation of the ambassador's Cretan subjects. Although Locke neglected the fact that Bingham's Cretan miners hated the Turkish ambassador almost as much as they hated Skliris, his attempt to harness resentment against the padrone was ultimately effective as hundreds of Greek and Italian workers soon joined the union.[25]

The depth of immigrant workers' anger took both WFM and company officials by surprise. On September 17, 1912, over one thousand immigrant union members voted to strike against the Utah Copper Company demanding higher wages, union recognition, and abolition of the padrone system. The next day, immigrant strikers were joined by hundreds of previously unorganized immigrants, including all two hundred Japanese immigrants, and succeeded in completely shutting down the country's preeminent copper mine. In addition to "digging breastworks and foxholes" and constructing a makeshift cannon, immigrant workers kept up continuous gunfire for over forty-eight hours over the heads of the small, but growing force of American deputies in Bingham. Strikers possessed every military advantage

[25]Utah, *Report of the State Bureau of Immigration, Labor, and Statistics, 1911-1912*, p. 30; *Official Proceedings of the 20th Annual Convention of the Western Federation of Miners*, Denver, Kistlet Stationary Co., 1912, p. 110, 117; Letter from E. G. Locke to "His Excellency the Ambassador of Turkey," in Washington, 5/12/12, William S. Spry Papers, Personal Correspondence, Box 19, State Archives, Salt Lake City, Utah.

and succeeded in intimidating the Utah Copper Company, local police deputies, and the National Guard from taking any military action during the strike's initial phase. Wrote the Salt Lake *Telegram*, "The strikers . . . from their position could with good marksmanship, good management and disposition of their forces, wreak destruction upon any force that might attempt to take them from the road."[26]

The impressive militancy of immigrant strikers reflected the powerful ways in which ethnicity and class overlapped and reinforced one another in Bingham. Ethnicity was a very visible part of strikers' militancy and ethnic groups formed the basic organizational building block of the striking work force. Yet, the militancy of Greek and other immigrant strikers represented far more than the retention and expression of particular ethnic traditions and temperaments. Strikers from quite different cultural backgrounds participated in fundamentally similar ways and for similar reasons during the strike effort. Strikers' gunfire had its ethnic antecedents in Italian banditry and Greek guerrilla resistance against the Turks, but was fueled principally by their shared class resentments against immigrant padrones and American managers of the Utah Copper Company.

The strength of immigrant workers' class solidarity was demonstrated at a dramatic open-air meeting of armed strikers, union officials, immigrant leaders, and Governor Spry, on the third day of the strike. Fearing a bloodbath between a growing army of over three hundred company deputies and over one thousand similarly armed strikers, Governor Spry and WFM president Charles Moyer agreed to hold the meeting in Bingham to discuss possible solutions to the military stand-off. Greek banker Nicholas Stathakos spoke first and appealed to his countrymen's sense of honor and patriotism: "For the glory of our nation, you should be law abiding here." Stathakos's appeals "deeply agitated" a great number of Greek strikers, however, and underscored the different meanings that *philotimo* possessed for laboring and professional Greeks. Unable to preserve order, Stathakos left the podium amidst a chorus of boos while Greek Orthodox priest Vasilios Lambrides attempted, with

[26]Salt Lake *Evening Telegram*, 9/19/12, p. 1; Deseret *Evening News*, 9/19/12, p. 1.

little success, to calm the angry strikers. A few minutes after Stathakos spoke, an unidentified Greek striker climbed onto the podium and began berating Skliris and the entire padrone system. His brief speech precipitated a series of emotional speeches by other rank-and-file Greek and Italian strikers, all of whom demanded that the Utah Copper Company immediately remove Leonidas Skliris and all other padrones from its payroll. The importance of this demand was highlighted by one angry Cretan miner who asserted that his countrymen were prepared to return to work without union recognition if Skliris were fired.[27]

Although scholars have interpreted this willingness by individual Cretan miners to return to work without union recognition as evidence of the underlying conservatism of Greek miners' ideology, Greek strikers were in fact strongly committed to the WFM and the struggle for union recognition. They demonstrated this class solidarity with other immigrant strikers shortly after the meeting with the governor, when Daniel Jackling, superintendent of the Utah Copper Company, announced that Skliris had resigned from the company. News of Skliris's resignation brought celebration throughout the breastworks in Bingham, but only a few strikers expressed any desire to end the strike. Two days after Skliris resigned, Greek strikers held a meeting in the WFM union hall to consider the possibility of returning to work. Discussion was "animated," but Greek strikers voted unanimously to continue striking for higher wages and union recognition. Greek workers were no longer merely protesting against the conduct of a bad padrone, but were united with other immigrants in their support for unionism and an end to the practice of labor contracting.[28]

Leonidas Skliris responded to the worst crisis of his career by wrapping himself in the paternalistic ideology that had once undergirded his power as a padrone. In a two-page letter printed on the day of his resignation in the Deseret *Evening News,* Skliris asserted that his Greek countrymen "loved him" because he alone was their true defender. Skliris's resignation letter conveyed a clear sense of betrayal and exemplified the ties of reciprocity that had once existed between himself and laborers

[27]Deseret *Evening News,* 9/20/12, p. 1, 3; Salt Lake *Tribune,* 9/20/12, p. 2.
[28]Deseret *Evening News,* 9/27/12, p. 1.

in Bingham. It also illustrated the profound ideological distance that had developed between Skliris and Greek workers. Skliris refused to believe that Greek workers were, in fact, committed to unionism and the complete abolition of padronism. Skliris had, in his own mind, always been a "good" padrone, providing his countrymen with jobs and job security at a fair and reasonable price. Rather than criticize his countrymen for being radical, Skliris instead embraced the idea that a Greek rival had conspired to take his rightful place as the protector of "his" Greek workers and concluded his letter by denouncing certain unnamed "vicious characters" who were "plotting machinations against my countrymen."[29]

Prominent members of Utah's elite Greek community, in turn, attempted to defuse the public perception that Greek strikers were radical. On the day after Greek workers voted to continue striking, George Photopoulos, editor of the Greek newspaper *To Fos,* stated in the *Evening Telegram* that "the Greeks in Bingham do not understand the significance of a union" and "are ignorant of such American customs." On the same day, Evangelos Skliris and Nicholas Stathakos announced the formation of the Panhellenic Union, whose purpose was to "establish schools where the Greeks can become familiar with the American language and customs . . . and to learn to respect the laws of America and in that way become more desirable citizens." Founders of the Panhellenic Union in Utah were committed to an upwardly-mobile, respectable type of Americanization, one that stood in direct opposition to the working-class form of Americanization that Greek workers had embraced with other immigrants by joining the Western Federation of Miners.[30]

Greek workers responded to these statements and actions with their own letter to the *Evening Telegram* three days later. Greek striker George Gatzouros, speaking for all of Bingham's Greek strikers, stated:

> We denounce all those self posed leaders of the Greeks once and for all and say that the Greeks have no leaders, except the state and national authorities; And we have

[29]Deseret *Evening News,* 9/23/12, p. 3.
[30]Salt Lake *Evening Telegram,* 9/30/12, p. 12.

to suggest to the would be leaders of the Greeks that it
is to their best interests to desist from making themselves
prominent and misleading the public regarding the strike
situation, or we will be compelled to show them up.

Gatzouros's letter captured the combative and boastful quality of
Greek strikers' militancy and underscored their abiding commitment to the struggle for union recognition. Despite the efforts
of Photopoulos and Stathakos to the contrary, Greeks continued
to work at the forefront of the ethnically heterogeneous strike
movement, manning the breastworks, searching trains coming
into Bingham for strikebreakers, and stockpiling whatever guns
and ammunition they could find. The efforts of Greek strikers
earned the praise of the WFM's union publication, *Miner's
Magazine,* which stated on October 3, 1912, that "the Greeks must
be given the greatest credit for showing the greatest spirit of
solidarity and discipline."[31]

Balkan Wars and Breaking the Strike

Just three days after Greek strikers voted unanimously to
continue the fight for union recognition, however, Greek strikers
were confronted with a crisis that sharply dramatized the tension
between their identities as Greeks and as striking laborers. On
September 30, 1912, the Greek government issued a general
draft order which recalled all soldiers who had served in the
Greek navy or army between 1900 and 1909. As Greek workers
throughout the Intermountain West enthusiastically began organizing themselves into military companies and training for
battle with the hated Turk, Greek strikers in Bingham faced a
profound dilemma. Should they betray their fellow workers and
countrymen on strike to fight the real Turk or should they finish
the fight against labor padrones and the Utah Copper Company?
Most Greek strikers eventually left Bingham to provoke angry
criticism from the *Miner's Magazine*:

[31]Salt Lake *Evening Telegram,* 10/2/12, p. 9; *Miner's Magazine,* 10/3/12,
p. 8.

> The Greeks who have gone back belong to the working
> class, and these men of labor . . . forget the conditions that
> drove them to the new world. . . . But the Greek, like the
> American, is moved by the sentiment of prejudice, which
> is commonly known as patriotism.

The editor condemned patriotic Greeks for fighting the wrong
war, but he overlooked the fact that without that "sentiment of
prejudice" Greek workers would not have rebelled against Skliris
and the Utah Copper Company in the first place.[32]

For Leonidas Skliris, by contrast, the Balkan War represented
a fortuitous chance to revitalize the padrone system and to restore
his tarnished credibility in both the Greek and American communities of Utah. As the self-appointed labor contractor for the
Greek government, Skliris welcomed those Greek workers who
could, in his words, "pay their own way home," but Skliris also
welcomed "those who have no money," though one wonders
what forms of "assistance" Skliris in fact proffered.[33] Adept at
bringing Greeks to Utah, Skliris was equally skilled in exporting
them in what was unquestionably a noble cause. Skliris made the
most of his rediscovered role as the patriotic spokesman of
Utah's Greek community:

> To be sure, the empire of the Ottoman is great and its
> soldiers are fierce and fanatic fighters but history has yet
> to show where the Caucasian race, with anything like
> equal numbers, ever went down to defeat in a war so
> important as this will be. The Turk is doomed.

Given Skliris's own recent experience with the union's "fierce
fighters," there was more than a touch of irony in his patriotic
sentiments.[34]

If the Balkan Wars helped Skliris reclaim his legitimacy in
the Greek and American communities of Utah, it likewise helped
the Utah Copper Company to break the strike by revitalizing

---

[32]Ogden *Standard*, 10/5/12, p. 12; *Miner's Magazine*, 11/7/12, p. 4.

[33]Skliris was joined in his patriotic crusade by several members of Utah's
middle-class Greek community, including Stathakos and Evangelos Skliris, who
organized several fund-raisers at the Greek Orthodox Church.

[34]Salt Lake *Tribune*, 10/22/12, p. 3.

the padrone system. On October 10, the Utah Copper Company imported one hundred Greek strikebreakers into Bingham in railroad boxcars provided by the Greek padrone Gus Paulos, a subordinate of Skliris. When Greek strikebreakers arrived at the Utah Copper Mine, they were confronted by hundreds of their angry countrymen who informed the strikebreakers of the strike situation and attempted to persuade them to quit. While their efforts seemed successful—over half of the Greek strikebreakers joined the strikers by the end of the first day—many of these newly-imported Greeks remained ideologically dependent upon Skliris. Because nearly half of the Greek strikebreakers remained on the job during the first day, the Utah Copper Company was able to start up three steam shovels in the mine.[35]

The Utah Copper Company also used armed force to break the strike. On the first day that Greek strikebreakers began work, an army of company deputies were well prepared for any resistance from immigrant strikers. When approximately two hundred Greek strikers prepared to prevent the strikebreakers from entering the mine works by force, fifty company deputies "swooped down" on the surprised strikers and arrested the Greek ringleaders Mike Louras and Jim Theros. Four days later, another preemptive attack by company deputies prevented twenty-five Greek and Italian strikers from accomplishing any "malicious mischief" against strikebreakers. As company deputies led the surprised strikers down the mountain, a nervous deputy shot Greek striker Mike Katrakis in the leg. In the ensuing skirmish, several Greek and Italian strikers received head injuries from deputies' gun butts.[36] Such brutal strikebreaking tactics proved to be extremely effective. By November 15, the Utah Copper Company had resumed full production with a completely non-union work force, many of them Italian and Greek strikebreakers imported with little interference from immigrant strikers. Swift actions by company deputies prevented many violent confrontations between strikers and strikebreakers from developing. More

[35]Salt Lake *Tribune*, 10/11/12, p. 8; Greek Oral History Collections, Marriott Library, University of Utah: Paul Borovilos, 4/1/70; Jack Tallas, 1/18/71; James Korobas, 10/3/74; Mrs. Isidore Kastanis, 3/2/73; Peter Argentos, 12/4/74; All five interviews conducted by Helen Papanikolas confirmed the same basic facts about breaking the strike with Greek laborers supplied by Gus Paulos.

[36]Salt Lake *Tribune*, 10/11/12, p. 1, 2; Salt Lake *Tribune*, 10/15/12, p. 3.

disarming than deputies, however, was the fact that Greeks and Italians faced their own countrymen on the other side of the picket lines. Unable to pit Bingham's immigrant groups against one another, the Utah Copper Company instead fragmented the solidarity of immigrant strikers from within each immigrant group. The importation of Greek and Italian strikebreakers was far more successful than force in dividing the powerful ethnic-based class solidarity of Bingham's immigrant strikers.

The company's tactic of pitting Greek against Greek and Italian against Italian also had its unforeseen consequences, just as the company's reliance upon the padrone system originally backfired with the 1912 strike. On the morning of October 25, from the hills above Upper Bingham, thirty well-armed Greek strikers opened fire on a startled group of deputies and Greek strikebreakers. After firing about five hundred volleys, the Greek strikers quickly fell back into the cover of the hills. Bingham Sheriff Joseph Sharp organized a massive posse, but was unable "to find a trace of the fugitives." Two weeks later, Greek strikebreaker Harry Spinborn died from injuries sustained in the surprise attack, the first Greek worker to die in Bingham's labor unrest. Many of these militantly class-conscious Greeks escaped to the coal fields of Colorado, where they encountered Greeks with similar convictions, such as Louis Tikas, future martyr of the infamous Ludlow Massacre of 1914.[37]

Conclusion: Greek Militancy and the Padrone

The larger significance of the Bingham strike lies not so much in its universal typically, but in its demonstration of the complex and dramatic ways that class and ethnicity intertwined and shaped each other's historical development in the American West. Class formation in Bingham was ethnic-based. The padrone-worker relationship was the principle mechanism by which immigrant workers comprehended their larger class identity. Western labor historians who dismiss the importance of the padrone-worker relationship and immigrant culture fail to comprehend how ethnicity nurtured the formation of militant labor protest

[37]Ogden *Standard*, 10/25/12, p. 13; Ogden *Standard*, 10/26/12, p. 12.

in the West. Likewise, they overlook the ways in which the padrone-worker relationship and immigrants' sense of patriotism undercut labor militancy. The Utah Copper Company divided the ethnic-based class solidarity of immigrant strikers by manipulating, with partial success, the ethnic loyalties of immigrant strikers.

Attempts to write the history of Greek immigrant workers that ignore the importance of class, in turn, miss a vital aspect of the history of both Greek workers and Greek professionals: the painful and potentially explosive accommodation of Greek culture along class lines to industrial America. Greek strikers were staunch supporters of the WFM throughout the strike and their militant actions exemplified the WFM's revolutionary commitment to a class struggle. Greek strikers did not possess an explicitly Marxist or revolutionary vision of society, but were nonetheless articulate reformers of a harsh industrial system, united with other immigrant workers in their demands that the Utah Copper Company eliminate the padrone system, increase wages, and recognize their union. These demands embodied their class position and class consciousness, but were also embedded within their sense of *philotimo,* a *philotimo* that was mutualistic, intensely political, and sharply divergent from the individualistic sense of *philotimo* that Greek professionals possessed. The Greek community of Utah's definition of ethnicity was the product of conflict and struggle, not merely with nativistic America, but also from within, as different classes of Greek immigrants demonstrated competing definitions of *philotimo* and Americanization.

Demosthenes Nicas: Labor Radical

DAN GEORGAKAS

One of the poorest documented areas of the Greek American experience is that of the Greek American left in general and Greek American members of the American Communist Party in particular. The reasons for this neglect are rooted in the McCarthy period and are similar to those characteristic of the histories of other ethnic groups in the United States. What became evident in the 1980s through specific studies covering events of the 1930s and 1940s is that prior to the 1950s there was a substantial Greek left whose activities have not been incorporated into standard ethnic histories. One difficulty in recovering this hidden history is that few of the Greek Communists have chosen to write memoirs or other accounts of their prime years. Even the most basic primary materials, such as pamphlets and newspapers, are hard to locate.[1] More often than not, what we know of the Greek left has come as a bonus from the scholarly study of a larger topic. Typical in this regard is the information on Greek fur workers which is usually derived from Philip Foner's *The Fur and Leather Workers Union*.[2]

[1]There is no archive in the United States devoted exclusively to the Greek left or even Greek labor. Occasional pamphlets or newspapers may be found in general collections of Greek material or collections on American radicals. The New York Public Library has a microfilm of scattered issues of the Communist press (*Phone tou Ergatou*, 1922-1923; *Empros*, scattered issues of 1926 and 1927; and *Empros*, sequential run: 1937-1938). The Poulos Collection of Taminent Library of New York University has material on Greek Trotskyists in the United States and abroad. The Greek Communists sent copies of all newspapers and other major publications to archives in Leningrad and Moscow. Whether these materials still exist has not been established.

[2]This work was commissioned by the union as part of its defense against McCarthyism and was published in 1950 by Nordan Press of Newark, New Jersey.

Given the state of affairs just outlined, the testimony offered by Demosthenes Nicas, who joined the American Communist movement at its birth and remained active throughout its heyday, is a major breakthrough. The account which follows is based on documents he has provided, public speeches, private correspondence, and several multi-hour taped interviews.[3] Nicas has examined the text which follows for accuracy, and I have checked his account against other existing documentation whenever possible. His story does not encompass the whole of the Greek American Communist experience, but it is an eye-opening introduction.

Demosthenes Nicas was born in Labove, Albania, a village sixty miles beyond the present Albanian-Greek border. Political instability in the area was chronic, and there was a tradition of Albanian and Greek immigration to Romania. During the last ten years of the nineteenth century and the first ten years of the twentieth century, the United States became increasingly attractive to would-be immigrants. In 1915, when he was approximately fifteen years old, Nicas immigrated to the United States, where his first permanent stop was Easton, Pennsylvania. He soon moved to Philadelphia to work as a busboy. After a few months of work, he noticed agitational postcards in the locker room. A Greek co-worker known to him only as Louie told him furtively that the cards came from the Industrial Workers of the World (IWW). Nicas recalls being told, "They are going to save us. This is the organization that is going to confront the capitalists and get us the eight-hour day and a week's vacation." Although just beginning to understand English, Nicas joined the IWW and occasionally went to meetings. He only understood a little of what was

Joanna Karvonides Nkosi's "Greek American Fur Workers in New York City, 1919-1954" was scheduled for presentation at the Saloutos Conference of 1989, but the author could not appear. Her text was not forwarded and apparently remains unpublished.

    [3]The original audio tapes of Nicas upon which this account is based were recorded in 1987-1989 and are available at the Oral History of the American Left project of the Tamiment Library, New York University. The 1987 tapes were made with the assistance of Alexander Kitroeff and the 1989 tapes with the assistance of Barbara Saltz. The spelling of names which follow in this text have been rendered to the best of Nicas's memory. In some instances the name may be a "Party name," but most are legal. Various letters, speeches, and comments on this particular text have been placed in a Demosthenes Nicas file at Tamiment. Nicas has been active in collecting primary materials on the Greek Communists and has helped facilitate their donation to libraries.

being said, but he liked the general orientation. Louie was the only other Greek in that local, which had an ethnic mix that included two Jews.

Louie decided to go to New York City in 1917, and Nicas followed shortly thereafter. They obtained work at various hotels and joined the Amalgamated Industrial Hotel Workers Union. Nicas states that there were two other hotel and restaurant worker unions. One of these was Local 1, which was limited to Germans and controlled the Wall Street restaurants. It had been organized in 1883 and had first belonged to the District Assembly of the Knights of Labor No. 49. The other union, Local 16, was organized during the Prohibition period and came under the influence of gangsters. The union to which Nicas belonged had a radical perspective. It had struck all the major hotels in 1912 in a successful walkout of forty-five days. Like all agreements made by the IWW or under IWW influence, the settlement was not formalized in a written contract.[4]

When the Palmer Raids struck the New York labor movement after the conclusion of World War I, Nicas decided to move back to Philadelphia where he was not so well-known to the local red squad. He had joined the Communist Labor Party that was led by John Reed, one of the two Communist parties which had emerged from the left wing of the Socialist Party in 1919. Partly due to the fear instigated by the Palmer Raids and partly due to other factors, the Communist movement remained underground for much of the 1920s. Membership in the organizations which founded the Communist movement in 1919 had been near 100,000, but that number dropped sharply in the underground period. Aside from the problem of sheer survival, the nascent movement spent much of its energy in leadership struggles, ideological debating, and negotiations to create a single national organization. The internecine battles disgusted Nicas. Like many other rank-and-file members, he paid his dues but did not attend many meetings.[5]

[4]The IWW regarded any one strike or settlement as only a stepping-stone to the new society. It believed that management would always scheme to get around obligations whenever it felt it was strong enough to do so. Having no contract left workers free to act at any time for more gains. Benefits already won would be guaranteed by the same worker solidarity that had won them in the first place.

[5]Nicas's major complaint was that debates on the theoretical principles of

As soon as Nicas received his citizenship papers in 1927, he returned to Albania through a voyage to Italy. His father had died, and he longed to see his mother. His sister, her family, and other relatives had moved to Greece. Neither nation seemed any more compelling that it had in 1915. Nicas was greatly troubled by the economic problems and the national trauma that accompanied the absorption of refugees from the lost war in Asia Minor. In March of 1928, he returned to Philadelphia.

The Communist Party (CP) to which Nicas returned had consolidated into one major above-ground organization of some 18,000 members. Of these, at least 500 were Greek-speaking. As the decade ended, the CP shed a right-wing faction led by Jay Lovestone (eventually Lovestone would become an anti-Communist advisor to the AFL-CIO) and a left-wing faction (supporters of Leon Trotsky) led by James Cannon. Nicas remained loyal to the formal CP, and in 1930 the District Committee of Eastern Pennsylvania appointed him to be organizer of the International Workers Relief in Philadelphia. Among his various duties he was to oversee Spartakos, a Greek workers educational club in Philadelphia, and, as he puts it, to "Clear it from Trotskyist, Lovestoneist, and anarchist elements."

Nicas's involvement with the workers club was characteristic of the assignments he would have throughout the decade and that others had in other localities. The primary purpose of the ethnic clubs was not recruitment of new members. The CP wished to have workers use the clubs as a social base and a point of political orientation. A core of party members would keep the clubs functioning and would use them to distribute party literature and agitate on social issues from a party perspective. In 1930, the Philadelphia club had approximately fifty regular members, of which only ten were in the CP. By 1935, there would be thirty such clubs, with some fifteen hundred members. These Greek clubs were concentrated mainly in Eastern industrial centers, a pattern typical of the entire CP.

The Greek workers' clubs could be thought of as political *kafenia*. Most of the political work was done verbally and even in one-on-one conversations. Backing this up were occasional

Marxism-Leninism were so time consuming and exhausting that there was little or no time left for union organizing or supporting strikes.

formal talks or community events. The most consistent form of persuasion was newspapers. From 1918 through 1953, the Greek American Communists maintained a press that was occasionally daily but usually weekly or biweekly. Top circulation came in the 1940s when some press runs might go as high as 10,000 but when the normal run was about 8,000.[6] Individual subscriptions were available, but many newspapers were sent in bundles to organizations or to organizers like Nicas. These organizers would then sell the newspapers to workers or pass them on to people they wished to influence.

Given the nature of the workers' clubs, the bundle system meant that there was considerable pass-on readership in which one copy was read by several people and discussions of issues might take place in a public setting. This was different from the single reader or family that subscribed to *Atlantis* or *Keryx,* the two Greek-language dailies.[7] The clubs also allowed the CP to get its views before those Greek workers who lived in rented rooms or were highly mobile. The Greek Communist press always used the Greek language, with an occasional column or section in English. The clubs, like the newspapers, remained immigrant-oriented and did not have many mechanisms for attracting mainly English-speaking, second-generation Greek Americans. The name of the party paper changed four times, each change indicating a shift in the party line, but the changes did not signal a shift in control. The papers were published in New York City and sent nationwide and to some international subscribers. The series began as *Phone tou Ergatou* (*Voice of the Worker*), 1918-1923; and then became *Empros* (*Forward*), 1923-1938; *Eleftheria* (*Free-*

[6]Various O.S.S. reports of the 1940s put the circulation of *Vema* between 5,000-8,500. See Elias Vlanton (compiler), "Documents: The O.S.S. and the Greek Community," *Journal of the Hellenic Diaspora,* Vol. IX, Nos. 1-4, 1982. Helen Christophorides handled the subscriptions at the time, including liaison with the post office, and she remembers the normal press run of the early 1940s as being 8,000 at its peak.

[7]*Atlantis* was royalist and *Keryx* republican. For discussion of the Greek-language press, see Dan Georgakas, "The Greeks in America," *Journal of the Hellenic Diaspora,* Vol. XIV, Nos. 1/2, 1987, pp. 10-14, and Constantine G. Yavis, *Propaganda in the Greek-American Community,* Department of Justice, April 21, 1944, reprinted in *Journal of the Hellenic Diaspora,* Vol. XIV, Nos. 1/2, 1987, pp. 122-129.

dom), 1938-1941, and *Helleno-Amerikaniko Vema* (*Greek-American Tribune*), 1941-1953.[8]

A major action led by Nicas in 1932 involved agitation against the Stefanou brothers, owners of a factory that made Ramses cigarettes. Some $20,000 had been collected by the community and was being held by Constantine Stefanou for the purpose of building a Greek school. Nicas organized twelve Greek societies into a united front asking that the money be used to help the Greek unemployed. After being denied so much as a meeting, Nicas decided to organize a demonstration in front of the factory. As soon as the plan became public, the chief of police sent officers to intimidate Nicas. Even within the CP faction of Spartakos, there was great fear. Nicas had to rely on a hard core of loyalists and some Albanians he had personally recruited and with whom he conversed in their native language. On the day of the action, hundreds of Greeks came into the streets. Nicas believes many of them came to see the Communists get beat up by the police. The large crowd, however, served to confuse the police about just who was a supporter and by moving his forces resolutely, Nicas was able to hold a successful three-hour rally. A few months later, there was a second demonstration. Although the Stefanou brothers grew more conciliatory, the money was never spent in the manner the united front had asked. But the bold CP initiative had won the respect of many Philadelphia Greeks. Membership in Spartakos surged and 150 new subscriptions were entered for *Empros*.

Shortly after the second demonstration, the Greek cargo ship Zephyros docked in Philadelphia. The union secretary of the ship and some of the crew visited Spartakos and gave out leaflets announcing openings for sailors and for a waiter to serve the engineers. Nicas thought this was an easy way of getting a trip back to Greece and he managed to get the waiter's job. The adventure which followed underscores the ethnic solidarity of the Greek workers of that era, the scope of Communist influence

[8]The first of these began as a publication of the left wing of the Socialist Party. The decision to cease publication was made in 1953, when the number of persons nationally available to assist editorially, make donations, and sell subscriptions had fallen to 100.

among Greek seamen, and the tenuous nature of the Communist network.

One of the first stops of the Zephyros was in Rosario, Argentina, where Nicas found a large and semi-organized Greek community. Some 100 to 150 Greeks worked in a Swift slaughterhouse in the area. Most of these men had families. At a meeting in a cafe which sold pastries and beer and coffee, the visiting seamen were asked to strike in support of a local action. A cargo ship that had preceeded them into port was under the control of a captain who was accused of having thrown his cabin boy into the sea. The sailors on that ship and their supporters on shore wanted to have the captain sent for trial in Greece. They thought a strike would move the Greek consul to make the necessary request of the Argentinian authorities. The effort to have the captain charged failed, but Nicas was appalled that the Greeks did not have contacts with Argentinians. Using a Greek who was active in the Argentinian Communist Party, he established a contact between the Greek community and Argentinian unions.

Nicas's activities in Philadelphia were known to the sailors and he was now asked to form a Spartakos club in Rosario so that the meat workers and seamen would have a place to gather informally and make any contacts necessary with their Argentinian counterparts. Nicas was made secretary of the club. He notes that the local activists in the club were Costas Agnostopoulos, John Spheris, John Fasollis, and Leandros "the Tailor." The club became the center of an effort to raise the pay for Greek seamen to that of other Europeans. Ten ships went out in what proved to be a successful strike. Shortly thereafter, Nicas was arrested by the Argentinian police on a trumped-up charge of attempting to shoot a captain, but Nicas was able to escape from custody and went into hiding.

From his sanctuary in the Port of San Nicholas, which was near Rosario, Nicas became embroiled in an attempt to organize the crew of the Lemmos. While discussing strike plans in a van, he was overheard by a Greek who provided food and supplies for the ships in port. This provisioner alerted the police and Nicas was arrested under a new charge of inciting to violence. Among the ships in port was the Mount Olympus, a vessel owned by

Socrates Onassis (the father of Aristotle Onassis), then general consul of Greece in Argentina. The crew of the Olympus went on strike in support of Nicas's release. He was set free on condition that he would be shipped back to Greece where a court under the control of General Metaxas was ready to try him for international subversion. On board ship he was beaten severely and had several teeth broken. Before returning to a Greek port, however, the Olympus was scheduled for a London stop. The seamen on board had only agreed to the terms offered in Argentina because of this stop. As soon as the ship left port, the Labor Defense of Argentina telegraphed its English counterpart, which was able to have Nicas taken from the ship as a political refugee when it docked at Graves End. Nicas was taken to the Waterloo Hotel to recuperate from his injuries. Two months later, comrades arranged for him to be shipped back to New York on the Majestic.

Upon arrival in the United States, he was greeted as a working-class hero. He visited the offices of *Empros* and met key personnel such as Peter Thailos and Nick Deleparaschos. He was soon in the field selling subscriptions. In Easton, Pennsylvania, he met the CP district organizer, who asked for his assistance. A Greek was married to a Polish woman who was very influential among the Polish workers in the Onondaga Silk Mills, which the party was trying to unionize. Nicas was asked to contact the Greek, who turned out to be a compatriot from the village of Labove. Nicas became active in the organizing drive and was arrested on a picket line as he was selling the *Daily Worker*. The judge who heard his case was moved to leniency because there had been no violence, but Nicas was ordered to leave the city. Although the police put him on a bus bound for New York, as soon as the vehicle crossed the Delaware River into Philipsburg, New Jersey, Nicas got off. He found an Albanian family that he had known for years, and they took him back into Easton the following morning. He worked another two weeks behind the scenes. With the new local in place, he was called back to New York City by what was now called the Greek Bureau of the CP.

The next months were spent at a party school where Nicas learned the fundamentals of Marxist thought and various organizational skills. Previous to this time, he had never read much aside from the *Communist Manifesto* and the party press. During the 1930s, he would read more. One title he was given was *Communism and Christianity*, which had been written by Bishop William Montgomery Brown in 1920. The bishop urged humanity "to banish Gods from the Skies and Capitalists from the Earth." Brown had been ostracized from mainstream Catholicism for his views, but his Christian socialism made him a world favorite of communists. His major work had been translated into Greek and published by the Greek Communist Party. The Communist Party of Greece also provided Americans with Greek translations of Lenin, Marx, Engels, and other favored authors.

After finishing the party school, Nicas was sent to organize clubs and study circles in New England. The year was 1935, and the party line was shifting to support of the popular front. Nicas formed at least a half-dozen groups. Among the towns he visited often were Lynn, Lowell, New Britain, and Haverhill. The structures he created were not designed to recruit individuals into the CP so much as to orient them to the principles of trade unionism. The majority of members were workers, but anyone could join. In Lynn, there were two doctors Nicas remembers with great respect and fondness: Dr. Constantides and Dr. Zervas, one from the Peloponnesus and the other from Samos. The atmosphere was one of total egalitarianism. Members took turns sweeping the floors and working in the kitchen. Nicas stresses that everyone was convinced that a new society could be created. All read *Empros,* and many of the clubs had modest libraries.

Times were hard, and Nicas often did not have enough funds to feed himself properly. Generally he slept on a table at the local workers' club. When the doctors in Lynn discovered he had no place to sleep and was not eating correctly, they opened their homes to him. Nicas believes that the reality of the Great Depression rather than abstract ideology was the major factor in the party's appeal. He says, "Starvation makes you progressive. Let me tell you one thing: when this [pointing to stomach] is empty, this [pointing to head] is full; but when this [stomach] is full, this [head] is empty."

Nicas was so successful in New England that later in 1935 he was sent to the club in Chicago, which was so rent with factionalism that it was in danger of dissolving. His first effort was to call a meeting of party members and, after resolving their differences, to work with them on the general membership. Among the ten or so people helpful in saving the club, Nicas believes that Theano Papazoglou-Margaris and her husband were most important.[9] In addition to writing a woman's column for *Empros*, Theano Papazoglou-Margaris was an actress. Working with her and against the initial doubts of many members, Nicas organized a theatrical performance in a hall with a seating capacity of 400-500. To meet expenses, the club members had to solicit advertisements from local merchants for the program notes to be distributed at the performance. This was done, and the play proved a successful event. The episode is noteworthy for the key role played by a Greek woman in resolution of a party problem.

While in Chicago, Nicas became friendly with a number of liberals. Although he was in and out of the city on his various projects, he maintained the contacts. Even earlier, he had attempted to forge a relationship with leaders of AHEPA (American Hellenic Educational Progressive Association), already the largest secular organization of Greek America. Given the size of the Greek workers' clubs, Nicas wondered if he could attend AHEPA conventions as a representative of *Empros*. He wrote to George Vournas and was told he could attend the 1936 convention. Nicas states that while he did not know all the AHEPA leaders, he came to know and like many of them. Most were New Deal liberals, and there were many issues they could agree on. He was not invited to private AHEPA meetings, but he was given complimentary tickets to open events, public dinners, convention proceedings, and the like. His approach to Ahepans was, "I am a Communist and you are a liberal. We are in a boat that is sinking. We can either work together to get the water out or we can drown separately." Major points of unity were opposition to Metaxas and distress over the Great Depression.

That Nicas was able to have cordial relations with some AHEPA leaders is not unusual for the time. The CP had abandoned its previous policy of emphasizing class differences in favor

---

[9]Nicas lists the following persons as activists in the club: Theano Papazoglou-Margaris, Babis Margaris, George Exarhos, Socrates Economou, Peter Parishiades, Ch. Christophilis, George Koutoumanos, Kosta Kostis, Rene Kokoshi, D. Birbilis, and G. Papageorgiou.

of a popular-front approach that sought to unite classes around democratic issues in the fight against fascism. The view toward groups like AHEPA was the same as that in the workers' clubs. As Nicas puts it, "We were not seeking to make a revolution but to build a trade union movement. We were not looking for members, but for influence."

With the rise of Hitlerism in Europe, the sentiment for liberal and radical cooperation swelled. At one point, some Chicago liberals asked Nicas what he thought it would cost them to buy one of the Greek dailies. He thought $55,000 would be a fair sum. The liberals approached the owners of *Atlantis* and *Keryx* but could not make a deal. Nicas then made a proposal that sounds incredible even half a century later. He suggested that the liberals consider becoming partners in the publication of *Empros!*

The arrangement—which had been approved by the Greek Bureau of the Communist Party was that *Empros* would cease to function as a purely Communist organ. The hammer and sickles would be removed from the masthead, and the paper's name would be changed to *Eleftheria.* The new editor would be Demetrius Christophorides, an editor at *Keryx* at the time. Christophorides was a Pontian Greek who had worked on various Greek publications and had been an editor of a Venizelist bulletin. He was not a Communist, but he was a man the Communists could work with. The new paper would pursue the policies of the popular front symbolized by Christophorides's editorship. All the principals agreed, and the merger was put into motion. The process took an unexpected turn with the signing of the Hitler-Stalin pact of August 1939, an agreement endorsed by the CP. The liberals withdrew their cooperation, unwilling to be identified with an organization that had called off, however temporarily, the struggle against Nazism. One lasting effect was that *Empros* did become *Eleftheria,* and Christophorides was to remain its editor, and then the editor of *Vema,* until his death in 1948. Among the Chicago liberals active in the ill-fated attempt to merge publishing efforts were John Mantas, Van Nomikos, J. Reccas, and Dr. G. Karaflos.

Nicas, an ardent supporter of the popular front, had other interactions with mainstream organizations which intersected with his efforts to create a mass movement against fascism and the Metaxas dictatorship in Greece. By 1936, the CIO under the leadership of John L. Lewis had begun to organize industrial workers. Reversing his harsh anti-Communist practices, Lewis now sought Communist organizers to help build the new union. In March of 1937, Nicas was in Steubenville, Ohio, renewing subscriptions to *Empros* and agitating Greek workers to join unions. He was approached by Clinton Goldman, a local leader of the Steel Workers Organizing Committee. Although Nicas's political ties were known, Goldman liked him and valued his organizational skills. Nicas was hired as an organizer with a salary of $25 week and $50 in expenses. He was told he could continue to sell subscriptions to the Communist newspaper.

For the next two years, Nicas would work for what became the CIO in eastern Ohio, western Pennsylvania, and a sliver of West Virginia. His region was roughly bound by Steubenville to Belle Aire on the west and Weirton to Wheeling in the east. He would spend one day here and another there unless a strike was in progress. When strikes did take place, up to 50,000 workers might be involved. Car caravans and roving pickets were part of the action. The battles were often violent. In one strike in which Nicas was present, workers and National Guardsmen were killed.

Nicas's activities were not confined to Greeks. He worked with all nationalities, but remembers particular contacts with Albanians, Turks, Serbians, Ukrainians, and Hungarians. His Greek and Communist ties were crucial to his work. If a town did not have a workers' club, Nicas would start his organizing work at the local Greek coffeehouse. He would seek to find a sympathetic person to use as his first recruit or he would ask that person to indicate who in the plant was essential to have as a member. Another tactic was to look up *Empros* subscribers at home. Again, the contact often just led him to another person rather than being the focus of the drive. The Greek reds and readers of *Empros* were likely to have an excellent sense about which workers were important to approach or to avoid at any given factory.

If Nicas's memories are as accurate as they appear to be, the majority of Greeks in the region where he operated were still industrial workers in the late 1930s. Even the merchants often had a working-class rather than middle-class consciousness, and they often operated family enterprises closely tied to the ethnic community. Nor is there any evidence that Greeks were resistant to unionism as stated in some early ethnic histories. During the landmark rubber strikes in Akron, Ohio, the Greek churches opened their doors to the strikers and fully supported the union. Nicas further notes that other organizers in the field also had deep radical roots. In Akron, for example, one of the Greek leaders was Panayotis Kajalias, who had been born in Samos. He had come to the United States at age 14 and soon joined the Socialist Labor Party led by Daniel De Leon. When the Communist Party was organized, Hajalias had left the SLP. One of his first CP party assignments was to organize textile workers in Bedford Mills, Maine. One can only assume there were sufficient Greek-speakers there to make such an assignment reasonable.

Nicas left the CIO in 1939 by his own choice. He wanted to put more energy into building the Communist Party, and he moved to New York City, where he became more directly involved in the publication, of *Eleftheria*. Nicas had also become romantically interested in Helen Christophorides, the daughter of the editor appointed in 1938. They were married in 1942.

Helen Christophorides Nicas has her own insights into the period. She notes that her parents were quite unusual in being very supportive of her desire for higher education. She was one of a handful of Greek women to attend Hunter College in the mid-1930s and was a founding member of the Artemis Club, the first Greek woman's organization on that campus.[10] She recalls the time as being artistically exciting for Greek Americans. She belonged to an informal social circle that centered on Michael Likakis. Theodore Stamos and Nassos Daphnis were also part of that milieu.[11] Her sister belonged to a dance company of young Greek women founded by Maria Therese Bourgeois, a former

[10]Helen Christophorides and a close friend initiated the club by obtaining a list of students from the registrar and contacting all those with a name that seemed to be Greek. She recalls that one of the women who appeared at the first meeting had one African parent and was very dark-skinned. The majority of women treated her so rudely that she did not return to subsequent meetings or activities. A full interview with Helen Christophorides Nicas is in preparation. When completed, a copy will be placed in the Oral History of the American Left project of the Tamiment Library.

[11]Stamos and Daphnis are among the four Greek American artists studied in *A Quality of Light*, a 54-minute documentary by Valerie Kontakos, 1990.

student of Isadora Duncan. The group performed traditional Greek dances as well as dances inspired by Duncan as interpreted by Bourgeois. They were so well received that impresario Sol Hurok was able to book them into Carnegie Hall. Most of the dancers were unmarried, and the company slowly disintegrated in the 1940s as the original members married or retired and insufficient newcomers came forth to take their place.

Another important activity of the time by Helen Christophorides Nicas was her service as editor of the English-language page of *Eleftheria* and then *Vema*. She also served as a record-keeper for the papers, with most of her efforts going into keeping the subscription records accurate. The economic situation for the papers was always grim. Pay was only $5 to $10 a week and highly irregular. The staff looked forward to the days when organizers like Nicas came in from their field trips with money obtained through donations and newspaper sales. "That's when we got paid."

The end of the 1930s produced yet another opportunity for liberal and radical cooperation when ethnic communities were disturbed by a wave of deportations. The specific issues had to do with allegedly fradulent or incomplete documentation, false papers, ideological concerns, and other specifics that masked what was simply anti-foreignism. AHEPA played an active role in defending Greek immigrants, and Demosthenes Nicas became active in the newly formed Committee for Protection of Foreign Born. Demetrius Christophorides was involved in a united front that went to then-Archbishop Athenagoras, who promised to help and did. Once the Nazis invaded both Greece and the USSR, Communists and liberals came to agreement on the issues of Greek war relief and aid to the armed resistance to German occupation.

Nicas's political activism was cut short in 1941 when he became ill with tuberculosis. He had to be hospitalized on several occasions and had to take regular work to support his new family. He was never again to be a full-time organizer even though both he and his wife continued to help with the newspaper as best they could. With the advent of McCarthyism in the 1950s, the FBI was at their door every week. Neighbors and friends were consistently told they were subversives. Demosthenes Nicas was harassed, blacklisted, and threatened with deportation. He notes with sadness that most of the Greek Communist leadership was deported at this time or forced to leave the nation to avoid jail. Some of these individuals had never become naturalized citizens, and all were vulnerable to McCarthyite pressure. Many rank-and-file members who remained in the United States become completely inactive or withdrew from political commitments for many years. Nicas believes that the collapse of the movement he had fought so hard to build was a matter of decapitation of the leadership by the federal government and intimidation at many levels of the rank-and-file.

The story of Demosthenes Nicas evokes the zeal and optimism of the radicalism of the 1930s. He indicates that for a considerable period, the Greek Communists often worked with mainstream community figures and organizations. His experiences strengthen the view that the history of Greek immigrants in the pre-1950s was quite similar to that of other Europeans who immigrated at about the same time. Large majorities entered the working class immediately upon arrival, and most remained in that class for the rest of their working lives. As workers, they overwhelmingly supported trade unions and the New Deal. A smaller percentage followed a more radical course or accepted more radical leadership. The Greek Communists never became as proportionally numerous or influential as their Jewish or Finnish counterparts, but they were on a par with the second tier of ethnic groups making up the backbone of the Communist movement. For over three decades, American Communists of Greek origin were able to maintain a national press and a political presence mainly based on the needs of industrial workers. Their movement remained primarily Greek-born and Greek-speaking. Unable to withstand the pressures of the McCarthy era, they had largely disappeared from public view by the end of the 1950s.

Ethnicity As Humanitarianism: The Greek American Relief Campaign for Occupied Greece, 1941-1944

ALEXANDROS K. KYROU

Immediately following Italy's attack on Greece on October 28, 1940, a spontaneous nationwide outpouring of compassion animated Greek American communities to organize local efforts to bring attention to Greece's cause and the necessity for financial and material support. Recognition of a need for a united national relief effort brought the leaders of the Greek American communities together in New York City on November 7, 1940. In addition to the varied local community leaders there were also present representatives of over 120 major voluntary associations, Archbishop Athenagoras with other archdiocesan personnel, and Greece's ambassador to the United States, Kimon Diamantopoulos. Guided by Athenagoras's proposals, the participating representatives unanimously agreed to unite in one Panhellenic and Pan-American organization to be known as the Greek War Relief Association (GWRA). They established the basis for the executive administration of the new organization, elected Spyros Skouras, the influential president of the National Theaters Company, as national chairman, set a financial goal of 10,000,000 dollars to aid Greece, and resolved to adopt a policy of political nonpartisanship. Two days after the November 7 meeting, New York State officially recognized the GWRA as an incorporated organization, and shortly thereafter the association was chartered by the United States State Department and formally empowered to raise and utilize funds for the relief of

111

Greece. Concurrent with its immediate administrative development, support for the GWRA gathered rapid momentum throughout the United States. By November 15 over 350 Greek communities and over 2,000 voluntary associations had joined the
GWRA; within a few months the GWRA had organized some
964 individual local committee chapters.[1]

In Greece, contrary to general expectations of a lightning
war and despite numerical and material superiority, the Italian
offensive launched from bases in Albania had been ground to a
halt; and, beginning on November 14, the Greek High Command launched a counteroffensive along the entire front in
Epirus and western Macedonia. The operation quickly succeeded
in driving the Italian forces out of Greece and was subsequently
carried across the frontier into Albania. In order to consolidate
unit advances and territorial gains the counteroffensive was halted
on December 28, by which time the Greek army was in control
of most of southern Albania. Italy's military catastrophe in
Greece and continued desperate defensive situation in Albania
had profound and irrevocably debilitating effects on Mussolini's
power and prestige; but of greater immediate import, Greece's
unexpected victories attracted Germany's strategic concerns. In
order to secure his Balkan flank before the impending attack
against the Soviet Union, Hitler intervened to rescue Mussolini
from Italy's widening fiasco in Albania by invading Greece and
Yugoslavia on April 6, 1941. By the beginning of June Greece
had been overrun and occupied by German, Italian, and Bulgarian
forces.[2] In response to the Axis occupation Britain immediately

[1]For information on the development of the GWRA and for details on the
organization's relief activities in Greece prior to the Axis occupation, see Demetrios J. Constantelos (ed.), *Agones kai Agonia: tes en Amerike Hellenikes Ortho-
doxou Ekklesias, Enkuklioi kai Eggrapha ton Eton 1922-1972* [Encyclicals and
Documents of the Greek Orthodox Archdiocese of North and South America
Relating to its Thought and Activity, The First Fifty Years 1922-1972] (Thessaloniki: Patriarchal Institute for Patristic Studies, 1976), pp. 281-297, 303-306,
passim; Greek War Relief Association, *$12,000,000* (New York: Greek War
Relief Association, Inc., 1946); Bobby Malafouris, *Hellenes tes Amerikes, 1528-
1948* [Greeks in America, 1528-1948] (New York: Isaac Goldman, printer, 1948),
pp. 218-226; George Papaioannou, *The Odyssey of Hellenism in America* (Thessaloniki: Patriarchal Institute for Patristic Studies, 1985), pp. 176-181; and
Theodore Saloutos, *The Greeks in the United States* (Cambridge: Harvard University Press, 1964), pp. 345-350.

[2]For detailed studies of the period involving Greece's early participation in the
Seconnd World War, see Mario Cervi, *The Hollow Legions: Mussolini's Blunder in*

sealed off all shipping lanes into Greece. The blockade was intended to deny the Axis any channels for supply and movement, but its implementation led, in part, to the rapid and widespread emergence of famine.[3]

With an average prewar annual wheat crop of approximately 750,000 tons, and a 1,000,000 to 1,300,000 tons annual wheat utilization level, Greece was compelled to normally import between 450,000 and 500,000 tons of wheat every year. The Axis occupation and the subsequent British blockade interrupted the normal means of securing the vital balance of wheat. The situation was worsened by the anemic grain harvest of 1941, which produced roughly 200,000 tons less than the prewar average. Furthermore, as domestic production declined, foodstuffs were held back in villages or vanished into black-market channels. The Axis expropriation of food stocks intensified the crisis, and the division of the country into Bulgarian, German, and Italian occupation zones disrupted the prewar systems of material dissemination and supply. The ingress of refugees into urban centers, especially the Athens-Piraeus area, further strained already acutely diminished resources.[4]

Reports of starvation in Greece began to appear in the Greek American press in early July.[5] The critical deterioration of

Greece, 1940-1941 (Garden City, N.Y.: Doubleday and Company, Inc., 1971); General Army Staff, *Ho Hellenikos Stratos Kata ton Deuteron Pagkosmion Polemon: Hellenoitalikos Polemos, 1940-1941*, Vols. I-V [The Greek Army During the Second World War: Greco-Italian War, 1940-1941] (Athens: 1966); Demetrios Katheniotes, *He Kiriotera Stratigike Phases tou Polemou, 1940-1941* [The Main Strategic Phase of the War, 1940-1941] (Athens: 1946); Costa de Loverdo, *La Grece au combat, De l'attaque italienne a la chute de la Crete* (1940-1941) [Greece at combat: From the Italian attack to the fall of Crete (1940-1941)] (Paris: Calman-Levy, 1966); Alexandros Papagos, *The Battle of Greece* (Athens: J. M. Scazikis "Alpha" Editions, 1949); Theodoris Papakonstantinou, *He Mache tes Hellados, 1940-1941* [The Battle of Greece, 1940-1941] (Athens: 1966); and Andrew L. Zapantis, *Hitler's Balkan Campaign and the Invasion of the USSR*, East European Monograph Series (New York: Columbia University Press, 1987).

[3]See John Louis Hondros, *Occupation and Resistance, The Greek Agony 1941-44* (New York: Pella Publishing Company, Inc., 1983), pp. 67-70; and Saloutos, p. 349.

[4]Karl Brandt in collaboration with Otto Schiller and Franz Ahlgrimm, *Germany's Agricultural and Food Policies in World War II, Vol. II: Management of Agriculture and Food in the German-Occupied and Other Areas of Fortress Europe, A Study in Military Government* (Stanford, California: Stanford University Press, 1953), pp. 235-238; Hondros, p. 67.

[5]*Ethnikos Keryx,* July 7, 8, 1941.

alimentary conditions in Greece evoked a surge of anger and frustration within the Greek American community that was analogous in scope and intensity to the nationalist euphoria which had followed Greece's refusal to submit to Mussolini's surrender demands in October 1940.[6] The Greek-language press was exceedingly vigorous in promoting the notion that effective action could be taken to loosen Britain's blockade and dispatch vital aid to Greece. Paramount in this movement was Basil Vlavianos, the publisher and editor of the *Ethnikos Keryx*.[7] Through a multitude of public appearances and his own newspaper's editorials, Vlavianos argued for the modification of Britain's blockade. Reflecting the basic sentiments of the Greek American community, Vlavianos believed Greece's resistance and its unique import dependency warranted qualifying considerations in regard to the implementation of Allied strategy. Vlavianos asserted that German propaganda would capitalize on a largely British imposed famine, and that fundamental humanitarian needs should be afforded greater importance among the Allies than temporal great power artifices. Vlavianos, therefore, concluded that Britain should permit and even lend support to a conveyance of relief supplies to Greece.[8]

Emboldened by Vlavianos's example and Greek press encouragements, Greek Americans throughout the United States began a campaign of telegraphing and letter writing to Washington, D.C., to enlist the sympathies of the United States government to influence British policy toward occupied Greece.[9] Efforts and pleas of this nature were characteristic of the undiminished, albeit frustrated, individual Greek American commitment to aid Greece; yet it remained for the collective strength of the GWRA to methodically and systematically overcome these new obstacles to relief. In contrast to other Allied relief efforts the GWRA

[6]Ibid., July 1, 22, 1941.

[7]For an analysis of the Greek Press in the United States, see S. Victor Papacosma, "The Greek Press in America," *Journal of the Hellenic Diaspora*, 5, no. 4 (Winter 1979), pp. 45-61; a cross-cultural examination of the press is discussed in Charles Jaret, "The Greek, Italian and Jewish American Ethnic Press: A Comparative Analysis," *The Journal of Ethnic Studies*, 7, no. 2 (Summer 1979), pp. 47-70.

[8]*Ethnikos Keryx*, August 9, 1941.

[9]Ibid., August 7, 1941.

remained committed to its goal of securing aid for Greece despite the nation's occupation by the Axis.

Pursuant to that objective, after outlining a relief strategy with the help of the executive director of the American Red Cross, Norman Davis, Spyros Skouras met with representatives of the United States State Department on August 21, 1941.[10] Supported by Davis and the United States' ambassador to Greece, Lincoln MacVeagh, Skouras presented a request to the State Deparrtment's Division of Near Eastern Affairs for a trial shipment of wheat to Greece. Skouras proposed that the GWRA, acting in the name of the Greek Red Cross, should charter a neutral vessel, load it with wheat in the United States or some other willing nation and dispatch it to arrive in Greece no later than early November. If the State Department considered it desirable, the GWRA would arrange to have a group of American citizens accompany the ship in a private capacity in order to supervise the distribution of the cargo. If the proposed shipment proceeded satisfactorily, the GWRA would follow it with others. Skouras additionally requested the assistance of the State Department in making the necessary preparations with the various belligerent governments for the passage of the vessel and the distribution of the cargo.[11]

With the understanding that neither the United States government nor the American Red Cross would be expected to take any part in the venture, the State Department's Near East Division favorably recommended Skouras's proposal to Assistant Secretary of State Sumner Welles. The Near East Division endorsed the GWRA plan for both humanitarian and diplomatic reasons. The Division's intelligence sources had concluded that the food crisis was more acute in Greece than in any other part of Europe and that it was commonly viewed that Britain, and secondarily the United States, had a distinct obligation to save a nation in the

[10]United States Department of State 868.48/1143, "Memorandum of Conversation," Shipment of food to Greece by Greek War Relief Association acting for the Greek Red Cross, August 21, 1941; United States Department of State 868.48/1144, "Memorandum," Proposed Shipment of Wheat to Greece by the Greek War Relief Association, August 22, 1941.

[11]United States Department of State 868.48/1144, "Memorandum," Proposed Shipment of Wheat to Greece by the Greek War Relief Association, August 22, 1941.

democratic camp from famine. Diplomatically, the Near East Division reported that the failure to send aid to Greece had created a perception within the Turkish government that the Allies had abandoned Greece to its dire fate after Athens had served their purposes to the maximum. Consequently, it was concluded that Ankara would not likely render any support to the Allied effort so long as the Greek exigency was met with indifference; more precisely, in view of the Greek example, the Turkish government's trepidations toward any Allied entanglements could be tangibly justified.[12]

Turkey's interest in Greece's plight opened an immediate conduit for the GWRA. While musing over the merits and feasibility of exerting leverage on Britain to lift its strategic blockade, the State Department assisted the GWRA in actualizing a temporary aid measure. The GWRA leadership had fashioned a second relief plan that was endorsed by the State Department, and ultimately accepted tactically by Britain, whereby food purchased by the GWRA in Turkey would be shipped to Greece and distributed under the supervision of the International Red Cross.[13]

Pursuant to its relief stratagem the GWRA began transferring funds to the International Red Cross in Geneva and to its own representatives in Turkey. The funds were to be used for the purchase of foodstuffs, vitamin concentrates, medical supplies, and eventually for the materials' transport to Greece.[14] Preparations for shipment, cargo disembarkation, and distribution were entrusted with a certain Delegate Brunel of the International Red Cross Committee in Athens. Acting under instructions from Geneva, and in concert with GWRA directives, Brunel sought the advice of the occupation authorities in Athens, and, with their consent, appointed an administrative committee of locally prominent philanthropists to deal with the tactical needs pertinent to the discharging and distribution of the in-

[12]Ibid.

[13]United States Department of State 868.48/1163, the London Embassy to the Secretary of State, Food Supplies for German-Occupied Territories, October 18, 1941.

[14]United States Department of State 868.48/1181, official Greek War Relief Association correspondence from Spyros Skouras to Assistant Secretary of State Breckinridge Long, October 15, 1941.

tended cargo.[15] Brunel also formed an executive steering committee consisting of, among others, representatives of the German, Greek, and Italian Red Cross organizations.[16] In a meeting held on October 21 the executive committee resolved "(1) to distribute foodstuffs (a) to hospitals, orphanages and other philanthropic organizations in the Athens district, (b) to public soup kitchens in the capital district... (c) to the islands of Syra, Andros, Hydra, Spetzai and the towns of Hermione, Chili, Halkis and Patras, and (d) to the population of the capital district; (2) to distribute gratuitously the foodstuffs to the people; and (3) to raise by voluntary contribution the money necessary to pay the cost of distribution."[17] Moreover, the executive committee garnered assurances of cooperation and assistance from representatives of the German and Italian occupation authorities and from the collaborationist Tsolakoglou government.[18]

A few days after the executive committee had outlined its relief priorities the steamship *Kurtulus* arrived from Istanbul and anchored off Piraeus. On October 26 the occupation censors authorized a communique to the press which stated that "the generosity of American relief organizations has made it possible to make distribution among the Greek population of large food supplies which have been purchased and transported from abroad."[19] The GWRA was not mentioned in the statement and the public at large apparently remained uninformed as to the organization's central role in the relief effort.[20]

The unloading and distribution of the *Kurtulus*'s cargo began on October 29. The occupation authorities honored their

[15]United States Department of State 868.48/1187, the Rome Embassy to the Secretary of State, Food Shipments for Greece from Turkey financed by the American "Greek War Relief Association," November 14, 1941; United States Department of State 868.48/1187, Second Secretary of the Athens Embassy, Burton Y. Berry, "Memorandum" (enclosure to No. 2510 of November 14, 1941, from the Rome Embassy), Condensed account of the preparation for and distribution of the first food shipment received from Turkey on the S.S. KURTULUS, together with an Annex showing in tabular form the quantity of foodstuffs distributed to the various types of organizations, November 14, 1941.

[16]Ibid.

[17]Ibid.

[18]Ibid.

[19]United States Department of State 868.48/1171, Special Assistant to the Secretary of State to the Greek War Relief Association, November 25, 1941.

[20]Saloutos, p. 349.

pledge to the International Red Cross Committee by facilitating the distribution of the foodstuffs. Furthermore, the Germans and Italians did not seize any of the shipment and actually assisted in preventing certain local criminal elements from availing themselves of part of the relief cargo. As an unprecedented venture in exceedingly acute circumstances the GWRA's sponsored shipment was a notable success; over 2,800,000 pounds of food had been distributed in Greece without Axis interference or expropriation.[21]

Some logistical problems arose during the course of distribution. An offer had been made to the International Red Cross Committee by officials of the collaborationist regime to unload the cargo from the *Kurtulus* and transport it to designated distribution centers. This service proved to be both dilatory and inconstant. Brunel consequently made other arrangements in preparation for any future shipments.[22] From the experience gained in distributing the GWRA shipment, Brunel and the executive committee resolved to direct more foodstuffs to public soup kitchens to enable them to double the number of persons served and to serve that number daily. Ultimately, Brunel also planned to extend the distribution to centers of intense need in other parts of Greece and to increase the stocks of hospitals.[23]

Once intelligence reports confirmed to the British that none of the shipment had been seized by the occupation forces, the GWRA was permitted to dispatch the *Kurtulus* on a second relief voyage. After taking on roughly 3,000,000 pounds of food purchased again in Turkey the *Kurtulus* arrived in Piraeus on November 10.[24] Thus began a regular procedure whereby food and medical shipments arrived in Greece during the early winter of 1941-42. During this period Brunel and his administrative committee overcame the logistical problems that had hindered

[21]United States Department of State 868.48/1187, Second Secretary of the Athens Embassy, Burton Y. Berry, "Memorandum," November 14, 1941; United States Department of State 868.48/1171, Special Assistant to the Secretary of State to the Greek War Relief Association, November 25, 1941.

[22]Ibid.

[23]United States Department of State 868.48/1187, Second Secretary of the Athens Embassy, Burton Y. Berry, "Memorandum," November 14, 1941.

[24]United States Department of State 868.48/1171, the Rome Embassy to the Secretary of State, November 15, 1941.

distribution following the first transport.[25] Most significantly, foodstuffs purchased from Turkey were sufficient to keep the public soup kitchens of the Athens-Piraeus area in operation from November 1941 to January 1942, feeding approximately 15,000 individuals daily.[26]

As the winter progressed Turkey's own domestic alimentary reserves became acutely diminished, and Ankara was consequently compelled to cut off all but a greatly reduced supply of food to Greece in January 1942.[27] Upon this development the GWRA sought the permission of both the British and United States governments to implement a proposal for the direct and unlimited purchase and shipment of food to Greece. London, however, objected to any direct shipment of goods to Greece if the intended relief materials did not originate in Turkey. This in-

[25]United States Department of State 868.48/1187, the Rome Embassy to the Secretary of State, Food Shipments for Greece from Turkey financed by the American "Greek War Relief Association," November 14, 1941; United States Department of State 868.48/1187, the Rome Embassy to the Secretary of State, November 15, 1941; United States Department of State 868.48/1171, in reply to SD 868.48/1171, November 14, 1941, Confidential Report for the Secretary of State from Joseph C. Green, Special Assistant to the Secretary in charge of the Special division, November 25, 1941.

[26]Hondros, p. 72.

[27]Ibid., pp. 68, 72. The potentiality of a wheat export shortage in Turkey had been foreseen by the GWRA as early as August 1941. With an anticipated decline in Turkish agricultural production, coupled with a Turkish governmental policy of low price-fixing which often led to hoarding by farmers, the GWRA had prepared an alternative contingency; United States Department of State 868.48/1143, "Memorandum of Conversation," Shipment of food to Greece by Greek War Relief Association acting for the Greek Red Cross, August 21, 1941; United States Department of State 868.48/1144, "Memorandum," Proposed Shipment of Wheat to Greece by the Greek War Relief Association, August 22, 1941. Shortly before the German invasion the Greek government had ordered and paid for approximately 50,000 tons of grain from Australia to cover the country's requirements through the summer of 1941. At the time of the Greek government's withdrawal into exile, the ships carrying the grain had reached Egypt, but they did not proceed any further. In concert with the GWRA's new contingency, the Greek government-in-exile planned to transfer the grain to Turkey where it would be used to replace wheat which the Turkish government, as it was understood, would then be willing to sell from not only its export allocations but also from its domestic reserves. Thus the flow of food to Greece could, pending British approval, continue through the channels established in Turkey by the GWRA; United States Department of State 868.48/1172, Telegram sent by the Department of State to the London Embassy, November 26, 1941; United States Department of State 868.48/1172, Wallace Murray from the Division of Near Eastern Affairs to Assistant Secretary of State Welles, December 3, 1941.

sistence was an outcome of a subtle schematic extension of Britain's strategic blockade and economic policy. Once it became clear that the *Kurtulus*'s relief supplies had not been seized in any part by the Axis, London was willing to further the relatively small scale exception to its general blockade policy on the basis of greater regional strategic considerations. In short, London initially permitted, and later encouraged, the shipment of relief supplies to Greece from Turkey in order to eliminate Ankara's surplus resources. More precisely, the British authorities feared that Turkey's resources might be utilized by the Germans. As a result, London favorably regarded arrangements which diverted Turkish foodstocks and goods to Allied nationals who would consume supplies that might otherwise become available to the Axis.[28] This having been accomplished the British were less responsive to renewed GWRA pleas for direct aid to Greece.

The frightful conditions of the occupation and famine reached overwhelming proportions in midwinter 1941-42. By early January 1942 reports began reaching the United States that as many as 1,000 persons were dying from starvation on a daily basis in the Athens area alone, and conditions were reported to be even more severe in some other centers.[29] Immediately, the Greek-language press, and virtually every other organized aspect of the Greek American community, increased the tempo of its insistence that food be sent to Greece at once and in enormous quantities regardless of any potential consequences to the immediate Allied war effort.[30] In this regard, the editor of Boston's weekly, *Ethnos*, concluded:

[28]United States Department of State 868.48/1172, report from the Division of Near Eastern Affairs to Berle, and received by Assistant Secretary of State Acheson, December 6, 1941. For a secondary source analysis of the importance of Turkish agricultural and mineral resources within a diplomatic and geopolitical context, see Selim Deringil, *Turkish foreign policy during the Second World War: an 'active' neutrality* (Cambridge: Cambridge University Press, 1989), pp. 21-22, 128-132.

[29]Office of Strategic Services, Foreign Nationalities Branch, Record Group 226, 14/GR-178, January 19, 1942. International Red Cross figures counted over 90,000 deaths throughout Greece during the winter famine of 1941-1942 (approximately 50,000 of which took place in the greater Athens area); for more details, see Hondros, p. 71.

[30]Office of Strategic Services, Foreign Nationalities Branch, Record Group 226, 14/GR-178, January 19, 1942.

It is therefore the duty of us all—the Greek press . . . our Church (archbishop and priests), the Ahepa, the Gapa, all our Communities, Organizations, and Groups and in general of every Greek, to make known to President Roosevelt and to the Government in London—with resolutions, telegrams . . . to DEMAND that the blockade of Greece be withdrawn and that the sending of food into Greece be permitted from every part of the world where it can be bought. There must be an organized effort on the part of all of us, of every one of us. This must be done now, immediately.[31]

In addition to nationalist motivations Greek Americans rose to the challenge of Britain's blockade because of individual humanitarian imperatives and deep personal distress; as a contemporary analyst observed:

Greeks in this country who see their relatives—fathers and mothers—dying in the Old Country are not satisfied with a promise from London that the problem has "sympathetic attention" and that the blockade may be released somewhat.[32]

Greek Americans were anxious to accomplish these relief goals and consequently further intensified their campaign to bring about the active intervention of the United States to expedite the lifting of Britain's blockade.[33] The Greek American press emphatically stressed that the United States possessed the necessary food and the ability to dispatch it. Implicit in the press' calls for the mobilization and concentration of efforts toward relief was the understanding that the issue depended totally on the public insistence of the Greek American community. What followed was a nationwide campaign in which communities and organizations lobbied elected officials in order to keep the issue before the government.[34]

Due, in large part, to the concerted Greek American lobbying

[31]Ibid., February 4, 1942.
[32]Ibid., February 4, 1942.
[33]Ibid., March 6, 1942.
[34]Ibid., March 23, 1942.

campaign and mounting intelligence reports the United States government became troubled by the situation created by the famine in Greece. Moreover, President Roosevelt and the State Department had substantive political misgivings regarding Britain's blockade policy. Apart from presumably alienating Turkey from any productive relationship with the Allies, the blockade gave German propaganda an unparalleled opportunity to attack Britain for what appeared to be the mercenary abandonment of a gravely imperiled ally.[35] The United States government was also keenly aware of the growing Greek American antipathy toward Britain and was duly concerned with its potential political ramifications.[36] Thus motivated, on December 3, 1941, the United States government asked London to supply information on its blockade of Greece and to confirm or deny allegations of responsibility for the famine. The British did not reply to the request and were therefore asked again on January 5, 1942, to provide a response to the United States government. A little more than a week later Foreign Secretary Anthony Eden dispatched a message exonerating Britain from any role of responsibility in the famine, and further stating that London's actions were being performed largely on the behalf of the Greek government then in exile. Eden's assertions, however, appeared disingenuous, for the Greek government-in-exile had earlier dispatched a series of desperate pleas to Washington, asking the United States to take direct action to alleviate the famine.[37]

Despite Britain's earlier resolve to maintain the blockade against Greece, by the end of January mounting world opinion and the ultimate realization of the full horror and extent of the famine finally induced Britain to reassess its policy. Accordingly, on February 22, 1942, London informed the United States government that it was willing to lift its blockade.[38] Additionally, and of immediate importance, the British government, along with the United States, agreed to a request by the GWRA for permission to charter a vessel to transport aid from America to Greece.[39] Thus empowered to undertake the provisioning of an

[35]Ibid., March 23, 1942.
[36]Ibid., February 11, 1942.
[37]Hondros, p. 73.
[38]Ibid., pp. 74-75.
[39]United States Department of State 868.48/3028, March 6, 1942; Office of

emergency relief operation the GWRA chartered the Swedish steamer *Sicilia*. Along with assistance from Lend Lease measures, the American Red Cross, and the philanthropic Medical Surgical Relief Committee of America, the GWRA amassed a cargo of some 2,500,000 pounds of flour, 9 tons of medicine, and 500,000 vitamin-concentrate units. The *Sicilia* left from New York on March 27 and relatively soon thereafter arrived in Piraeus where its relief supplies alleviated the immediate crisis.[40]

The success of any long-term strategic relief program for occupied Greece, however, required the concordant approval and participation of the key belligerents. Cognizant of this need and after considerable inquiry and planning, the GWRA devised a relief proposal which it dubbed "Operation Blockade." Resurrecting and modifying the organization's earlier relief overtures, Operation Blockade proposed the utilization of a neutral party to convey cargoes of food, medicine, and clothing to Greece provided that safe passage could be assured from the belligerent nations. Following deliberations with President Roosevelt, Under-Secretary of State Welles, and Red Cross Chairman Davis, the GWRA leadership expanded the outline of their proposal by incorporating the former individuals' suggestions to employ a neutral commission within Greece which would conceivably insure the proper distribution of relief supplies.[41] In this regard, the *Kurtulus* relief period had provided the ideal experiential antecedents for such an international arrangement.

The GWRA held that the earlier connections developed between Britain and the occupation authorities through the International Red Cross could be further utilized to forge a mutual accord to expedite even more substantive relief measures. Pursuant to the actual material requirements involved in Operation Blockade the GWRA reserved funds for the plan's implementation, began soliciting wheat and other alimentary donations from concerned governments, and entered into negotiations with rep-

Strategic Services, Foreign Nationalities Branch, Record Group 226, 14/GR-178, March 17, 1942.

[40]Greek War Relief Association, *A Statement by the Greek War Relief Association, Inc. to its Chapters and Co-Workers* (New York: Greek War Relief Association, Inc., 1943); Malafouris, p. 221.

[41]Saloutos, p. 349.

resentatives of a sizeable fleet of immobilized Swedish vessels.[42]

Britain accepted the outline of Operation Blockade in principle, but concern over the potential political and strategic repercussions of lifting the blockade led London to insist that neutral Sweden appear as the originator of the relief initiative.[43] The GWRA, completely immersed in bringing Operation Blockade to fruition, therefore deferred public attentions to Stockholm.[44] On March 2 London and Washington formally invited the Swedish government to undertake the relief program. Stockholm accepted the project and on March 19 the Swedish Foreign Minister, Erik Boheman, and Prince Karl, Chief of the Swedish Red Cross, proceeded to contact the Axis. The Italians responded favorably on April 7, and Rome's acceptance was followed by an even more positive reply from Berlin on April 27. Rapid implementation of the program was forestalled only by differences over the structure of the necessary relief commission.

The German and Italian governments assumed that the existing International Red Cross authorities in Athens, which were in charge of relief operations in Greece since the *Kurtulus* period, would continue to direct the distribution of any additional relief. The British government, openly resentful and distrustful of the International Red Cross apparatus, demanded that the original committees in Athens be disassociated from any larger relief operations and that Swedish authorities be given sole responsibility for the execution of the program. Neither party showed any inclination to compromise and the relief deliberations reached an impasse which lasted until the beginning of August. Under pressure from the United States the British government accepted a compromise plan drafted by Foreign Minister Boheman to establish an Action Committee tentatively composed of Greek and Swedish personnel. The new committee would be solely responsible for relief distribution while the original International Red Cross Committee would continue to operate but only as a

[42]For information on the specific use of the Swedish vessels eventually employed in Operation Blockade, see Malafouris, p. 222.

[43]Hondros, p. 74; United States Department of State 868.48/3157, "Memorandum," June 13, 1942; United States Department of State 868.48/3168, the London Embassy to the Secretary of State, June 30, 1942.

[44]At this point the GWRA's "Operation Blockade" proposal became known as the "Swedish Plan"; see Hondros, p. 74.

liaison between the Action Committee and the Allies and Axis.[45]

The Action Committee quickly developed into what became officially known as the Joint Relief Commission during the month of August 1942. The headquarters of the Commission were established in the Marasleion School of Archeology in the Kolonaki district of Athens and a Swedish national, Emil Sandstrom, was eventually appointed organizational president by the Swedish government to act on behalf of the Swedish Red Cross. The relief apparatus was coordinated between two supreme centers: the Athens general headquarters, employing approximately 500 local citizens, which was organized to handle the allocation, distribution, and basic control of shipments; and the Piraeus office, employing some 130 Greeks, which supervised the unloading of relief shipments, the processing of wheat into flour, transportation within Attica, Piraeus, and other prefectures, and the storage and maintenance of relief goods and depots respectively.[46] The Athens headquarters functioned through five management and operational sections: the Office of the President, Documentation and Coordination, Accounts, Distribution to the Capital and Provinces, and Medicine and Children. The fourth section, Distribution to the Capital and Provinces, was divided into two regional divisions (one for the Athens-Piraeus area and one for the provinces) to more effectively regulate the distribution of ration cards and commissary allotments.

In order to insure proper relief apportionment each division was assigned a verification unit charged with the inspection and control of distribution, and the units were further empowered to prosecute any infringements of the Commission's regulations.[47] The division for provincial distribution maintained representa-

[45]Hondros, p. 74-75; United States Department of State 868.48/4892, Board of Economic Warfare, Blockade and Supply Branch, Reoccupation Division Confidential Report, *Greece: Relief Food Distribution by the Joint Relief Commission,* June 12, 1943; United States Department of State 868.48/3157, "Memorandum," June 13, 1942.

[46]United States Department of State 868.48/4892, Board of Economic Warfare, Blockade and Supply Branch, Reoccupation Division Confidential Report, *Greece: Relief Food Distribution by the Joint Relief Commission,* June 12, 1943.

[47]Ibid. For local case examinations of the administration and operations of the relief apparatus, see Philip Argenti, *The Occupation of Chios by the Germans and Their Administration of the Island, 1941-1944* (Cambridge: Cambridge University Press, 1966), pp. 170-175, *passim;* and Greek War Relief Association, *A Letter from Issari* (New York: Greek War Relief Association, Inc., 1943).

tives and major relief centers in Kalamata, Patras, Thessaloniki, and Volos on the mainland. The supervision of distribution on the islands was administered by a stationary representative in Crete and by two mobile representatives which were detailed to travel between Chios, Mytilene, and Samos. Lastly, at the most basic level some 1,600 local subcommittees in towns and villages were organized to handle the outmost distribution of foodstuffs sent to their respective areas by the Commission.[48] All totalled, by late 1942 the Joint Relief Commission included 25 executive Swedish and Swiss officials, over 1,200 Greek employees, approximately 3,000 local volunteers, 5 Swiss and 42 Greek physicians, several Swiss nurses, over 1,000 ancillary Greek medical volunteers, and a motorized pool of approximately 100 major transport vehicles.[49]

As the Joint Relief Commission developed its administrative and operational apparatus the GWRA, and its Commonwealth counterpart, the Greek War Relief Fund of Canada (GWRF), requested and obtained a substantial relief donation of 15,000 tons of wheat from the Canadian government.[50] The GWRF also purchased 50 tons of medical supplies from the American Red Cross. These collective relief materials were assigned to three Swedish vessels which left Montreal for Greece on August 7, 1942.[51]

With the dispatch of relief supplies in August, aid shipments became regular and systematic thereafter. Steady shipments originating in both Canada and the United States were carried on a monthly basis by a fleet of eight, and later twelve, Swedish vessels.[52] From August onward the relief project provided for

[48]United States Department of State 868.48/4892, Board of Economic Warfare, Blockade and Supply Branch, Reoccupation Division Confidential Report, *Greece: Relief Food Distribution by the Joint Relief Commission,* June 12, 1943.

[49]Ibid.; Brandt, Schiller and Ahlgrimm, p. 240.

[50]Malafouris, p. 222; For information on the GWRF, see Florence MacDonald, *For Greece a Tear, The Story of the Greek War Relief Fund of Canada* (Fredericton, New Brunswick: Brunswick Press, 1954).

[51]Ibid. United States Department of State 868.48/4892, Board of Economic Warfare, Blockade and Supply Branch, Reoccupation Division Confidential Report, *Greece: Relief Food Distribution by the Joint Relief Commission,* June 12, 1943; United States Office of Strategic Services, Foreign Nationalities Branch, 14/GR-178, April 24, 1942.

[52]United States Department of State 868.48/4892, Board of Economic War-

a regular minimum monthly shipment of 15,000 tons of wheat, 3,000 tons of dried vegetables, 100 tons of powdered milk, and other materials.[53] The costs of the purchased supplies and transportation were assumed in the main by the GWRA and the Greek government-in-exile. Eventually, the GWRA and the GWRF were successful in gaining the regular financial and material support of the American Red Cross, the Canadian government, the United States government through Lendlease provisions, other charitable governments and charitable organizations.[54] With these resources and support the Joint Relief Commission operated vigorously and with consummate success during the remainder of the occupation and through the first months following liberation. By March 7, 1945, the GWRA had dispatched 101 individual fleet shipments to Greece which delivered 647,153 tons of wheat and other foodstuffs, 2,878 tons of clothing, and 19,601 tons of medicine and related supplies.[55] The GWRA's Operation Blockade thus prevented a repetition of the catastrophic winter famine of 1941-42 on a larger scale during the following two winters of occupation. Estimates in the summer of 1942 anticipated 1,000,000 deaths for that coming winter without the arrival of any external relief.[56] The Greek American community's undaunted concern for the plight of the homeland, the political corollary of which was the concerted advocacy and agitation for the permutation of Allied strategic policy, assured the intrinsic mortal survival of Greece.

fare, Blockade and Supply Branch, Reoccupation Division Confidential Report, *Greece: Relief Food Distribution by the Joint Relief Commission,* June 12, 1943.

[53]Ibid. Shortly before liberation, during the summer of 1944, the GWRA transport fleet was increased to sixteen ships and the monthly importation of foodstuffs had risen to approximately 35,000 tons; see Brandt, Schiller and Ahlgrimm, p. 240.

[54]Ibid., Hondros, p. 75.

[55]Malafouris, p. 222.

[56]Greek War Relief Association, *$12,000,000,* pp. 6-7; Hondros, p. 75; Saloutos, p. 350; United States Department of State 868.48/3136, Assistant Secretary of State to President Roosevelt, April 15, 1942.

Greek American Literature: Who Needs It?

Some Canonical Issues Concerning the Fate of An Ethnic Literature

YIORGOS KALOGERAS

To mention Greek American literature is to prepare oneself at best to answer whether Nikos Kazantzakis's work qualifies as Greek American, at worst, to face a blank expression of incomprehension or a patronizing pat on the back. In other words, the Greek American literature scholar has, of necessity, to undertake an "archeological" expedition which will establish the "genealogy" of his subject as well as the legitimacy of the subject's status. Just how misunderstood such an undertaking has been over the years can very well be demonstrated with reference to the early attempts to establish a Greek American canon. Michael Cutsumbis's pioneer bibliography (1970) includes a section titled "Greek Americans in Fiction"; consequently, Peter Sourian's *Miri* (1957), that is, an Armenian American novel with a Greek subject-matter, is listed along with H. M. Petrakis's and Maria Vardoulakis's books; moreover, it contains Konstantinos Rhodokanakis's *Forever Ulysses* (1938) although this novel is a translation from the Greek.[1] On the other hand, Alexander Karanikas's *Hellenes and Hellions: Modern Greek Characters in American Fiction* (1981) discusses Petrakis's Leonidas Matsoukas along with Carson McCullers's Antonapoulos and Xaviera Hollander's Greek "customers." Further attempts by

[1]Michael Cutsumbis, *A Bibliographic Guide to Materials on Greeks in the United States* (Staten Island, New York: Center for Migration Studies, 1970).

Karanikas (1983) sort out the Greek American writers more carefully but remain limited because of lack of space; George Giannaris's book, *The Greek Immigrants and the Greek-American Novel* (1985), brings back the confusion by including indiscriminately Greek American writers and Greek characters in American fiction. My own work attempts to present the first comprehensive catalogue of texts written by Greek Americans both in English and in Greek (1984, 1985, 1987).[2] However, it remains incomplete since it does not include plays and it evinces a certain amount of discomfort as to which texts by which living Greek American writers, who publish in Greek and in English, ought to be included.

Some explanations should be given for the quandary facing the scholar of Greek American literature. Language remains the most thorny issue; is English *the* language of Greek American literature? If so, a large number of Greek texts published in the U.S. ought to be excluded. Naturally, such an exclusion deprives Greek American literature of its legitimate beginnings and delegitimizes completely important writers such as Theano Papazoglou-Margaris. Furthermore, it relegates to silence a large segment of the first immigrant generation and justifies scholarly misconceptions concerning the immigrants' lack of literary aspiration. If English *is* the language of Greek American literature, then its literary history should begin with Demetra Vaka-Brown and then move on to Maria Vardoulakis and the second generation.

A second set of questions relates to the content and the form of the texts to be included in the canon. What is the ideological function that formal and subject-matter choices postulate? Is Greek American literature simply popular literature? Is ethnic content an index of authenticity? What then of works which lack ethnic content? Moreover, what of those works which focus exclusively on Greece without the slightest reference to the U.S.? Are those to be brought within the fold of Greek American literature or to be relegated to a never-never land of ethnically "unmarked" texts?

[2]Yiorgos Kalogeras, *Between Two Worlds: Ethnicity and the Greek American Writer* (Tempe: Arizona State University, Ph.D. dissertation, 1984); "Greek American Literature: An Introduction and a Bibliography of Personal Narratives, Fiction and Poetry." *Ethnic Forum* 5 (Fall 1985): 106-128; "Greek-American

Still a third cluster of questions concerns what Cutsumbis, Karanikas, and Giannaris tried to come to terms with either explicitly or implicitly. They all pointed toward the idea of a "healing" or "consolidating" process which might situate certain texts by Greek American writers within American literature.[3] However, such an attempt simply glosses over the standardizing processes of mainstream establishment; furthermore, it validates the establishment's ideology concerning the "pathology" of the "other" in American literature. The consensus the aforementioned critics agree upon valorizes the dominance of the eternal classics in American literature; dissensus is perceived by implication as "militant" commitment to partiality—sectarian, closed, narrowly programmatic.[4]

A proper "genealogy" of Greek American literature ought to begin with the text which chronologically establishes its beginning. The question is which beginning? There is an English text, *The Personal Narrative of John Stephanini, a Native of Arta* (1827) and a Greek one, Konstantinos Kazantzis's *Istoriai tis Patridos mou* (1910). Are we to consider language the determining and unifying factor and consequently establish two different canons, the Greek American and the Greek-in-America ones? Yet if Stephanini's claim is true, that is if his book is a translation from the Greek, then Greek American and Greek-in-America beginnings coincide in an ür-text, now possibly lost. This goes a long way toward showing how specious the language question is and how in establishing a canon we must use other criteria.

I believe that we must focus on how much Stephanini relies on the paradigm of the American captivity narrative in structuring his text. He appropriates the ideological function of it, emphasizing not *white* resilience and survival in wilderness, but Greek (synonymous to civilized) resilience and survival in the midst of Turkish barbarity. Furthermore, he points out that America can reinforce resilience and expedite survival when he

Literature: An Essay and a Bibliographic Supplement." *Ethnic Forum* 7 (Spring 1987): 102-115.

[3]Annette Kolodny, "The Integrity of Memory: Creating a New Literary History of the U.S." *American Literature* 57 (May 1985): 292.

[4]Sacvan Bercovitch, "America as Canon and Context: Literary History in a time of Dissensus." *American Literature* 58 (March 1986): 107.

forcefully states that the profits from the book's sale will ransom his family from the Turks.

Paramount in Kazantzakis's text, *Istiriai tis Patridos mou*, is the use of the Greek vernacular culture as that reflects on the form and the content of the collection's five stories. We should not forget the ideological import such use implied. On the one hand, it was a polemical gesture on the side of Greek demoticists; on the other, it was an affirmation of the unity of Greek culture, an idea that had come under attack in the nineteenth century. Within the context of the immigrant community of Chicago such a text reassured the nationalistic feelings of the immigrants facing discrimination and downright racism in the Midwest. It provided them with a reminder of the continuity of the Greek race, a reminder which was natively published and not imported from the pre-American motherland. Lastly, it countered the allegations that the immigrants were "Mediterranean niggers," uncouth barbarians in search of a "million green dollars" alone.

Therefore, the originating textual acts of the Greeks in the New World, whether in Greek or in English, become acts of deep ideological importance. In this, the circumstances of textual production and dissemination within a specific culture, the American, are far more significant than the language used in order to determine the unity of these texts under the rubric of Greek American literature. Furthermore, it is important to understand that Demetrios Valakos's *Tragoudia tis Patridos mou* (1912) and Aristidis Phoutridis's *Lights at Dawn* (1918) belong to the same canon, not so much because they both harken back to the poetic influence of Palamas, but because they were produced and had relevance within the context of the immigrant community of the New World.

The relationship between ideology and form should alert the reader to look beyond the oversimplistic evaluations of early Greek American writing altogether. The issue of cryptoethnicity, for example, informs not only the thematic transformations of the text, but it affects its form as well. A perfect example that validates this claim is the work of Demetra Vaka-Brown (1877-1946). Her numerous novels and personal narratives, almost completely forgotten today but well received in her day, betray inherent irreconcilable ideological tensions which reflect on the content and the form of the texts. Furthermore, they suggest a sophisticated dissensus which far transcends their characterization by the critics as simplistic popular literature. Thus characterized and classified, Vaka-Brown's books have remained an embarrassment for the Greek American literature scholar rather than an example of interesting ideological questioning of the American Dream.

Vaka-Brown freely uses both the realistic and sentimental modes of writing, situating herself within the predominant literary traditions of the U.S. Her books are romances as well as historical travelogues that take their narrator through her native Orient; they are what Nina Baym identified as woman's fiction and at the same time "realistic" depictions of life in the Orient.[5] Yet through the ideological gesture of the appropriation of form Vaka-Brown seeks to expedite Greek nationalistic projects and to make a pithy statement concerning an immigrant woman's relation to her ethnicity and to the American Dream. A constant steering among forms and modes of expression characterizes these texts which appear to seek legitimation through this perpetual act of formal/expressive appropriation. It is an act of appropriation, however, which walks the thin line between the ideological assumptions of the two sides of identity. This "walking the line" shields the narrator from potential attacks concerning the authenticity of her projects. American and Oriental/Greek are adequately vindicated by the constant shifting and changing of expressive modes and by the alternation of forms, but also by the conscious reworking and rewriting of forms and expressive modes. Increasingly and imperceptibly, history, realism and autobiography, the discourse of the real, are associated with the narrator's American experience; on the other hand, romance, folklore, sentimentality, fantasy, the discourse of desire, become expressive of her Oriental/Greek experience.[6] The former legitimizes "Demetra" as American, whereas the latter marks her as Greek/Oriental. Both are constitutive of her identity. Yet the discourse of desire is associated with emotional fulfillment and psychic release, while the discourse of the real

[5]Nina Baym, *Woman's Fiction: A Guide to Novels by and about Women in America 1820-1870* (Ithaca and London: Cornell University Press, 1978): 11-12.
[6]Elizabeth Ordonez, "Narrative Texts by Ethnic Women: Rereading the Past, Reshaping the Future." *MELUS* 9 (Winter 1982): 20.

translates into ideological security, albeit personal frustration. In short, Vaka-Brown's work introduces a series of issues and raises a multiplicity of questions too complex to be answered simply by referring to an "anxiety of legitimation," or by relegating her work to popular fiction.

Demetra Vaka-Brown's work was relegated to silence and was dismissed as popular fiction unworthy of critical attention. In her case, failure on the part of the critic to recognize the complex ideological allegiances her texts attempted to articulate resulted in her dismissal. In the case of Harry Mark Petrakis's reading, his ideological choices in a limiting manner also resulted in the diminution of one of his better books. Petrakis had already produced two novels and a book of short stories which was nominated for the National Book Award (1965) when *A Dream of Kings* appeared (1966). The book became a national bestseller both in the hardbound and paperback editions, fulfilling one of the two prerequisites which according to Richard Ohmann go into the making of a canonical work.[7] The second prerequisite, however, proved unattainable as critical response remained condescending. The real problem for the book was the unfortunate comparison with Kazantzakis's work it elicited. For critics this was "Zorba the Greek American," which meant that the book was measured up not against *Alexis Zorbas* but against Cacoyannis's immensely popular movie *Zorba the Greek* (1964).[8] Naturally, the movie worked with images and music to build the dionysiac, carnivalesque essence of a character who is sustained and functions within Cretan popular culture. The success of the movie guaranteed the abstraction and reification of these images and music and their elevation into a national stereotype. Petrakis's character was perceived as an awkward attempt to flesh out this stereotype in American terms and to win for its creator a position within American literature as an ethnic writer who represents the Greek American community. In other words, the book was seen as an attempt on Petrakis's part to legitimate himself as the Greek American writer *par excellence* by appropriating the Zorba stereotype. At worst, then, the critics saw

[7]Richard Ohmann,, "The Shaping of a Canon: U.S. Fiction 1960-1975." *Critical Inquiry* 10 (September 1983): 206.

[8]Daniel Stern, "Zorba the Greek American." Review of *A Dream of Kings* by Harry Mark Petrakis. *Saturday Review* (October 1966): 63-64.

Leonidas Matsoukas as a stereotype, and they did so because they
assumed that it was based on a stereotype. At best, they saw him
as a literary image replicating the image of *the ethnic* the Jewish-
American writers had already created in the 1950s and the 1960s.[9]
In the eyes of many, the book simply affirmed either that ethnic
means popular and therefore less serious, or that ethnic specificity
is expendable in favor of a more general paradigm. The book
became an unsuccessful popular movie starring Anthony Quinn
and Irene Papas and then disappeared permanently both from
the critical and the public eye.

If *A Dream of Kings* was denied status, Nicholas Gage's
Eleni (1982) was given representative status within American
literature. The book was canonized because it was read as a
specific ideological gesture on the part of the narrator/writer
pleasing to the critics. It was considered the work of a "brilliant
sociologist"; "it called to mind classical tragedy"; "it was the
tender testimonial of a son's love for his mother."[10] The book
sold well and received excellent reviews, fulfilling the two prerequisites for canonization. However, what the reviewers sup-
pressed was how the book built on and affirmed the West's/
America's fears of its political "other," communism. Moreover, it
did so in the days of the "evil empire" and "America's backyard"
rhetoric. On a different level, what was intentionally overlooked
was that the book was the narrator's *auto-da-fé*, the spiritual testament of an immigrant's Americanization, an Americanization
that translated into unthinking reaffirmation of the American
Way and Cold War propaganda. Like *A Dream of Kings*, however, the movie made from the novel proved to be a commercial
and critical failure.

Eleni was canonized as a text which legitimized certain political choices of the mainstream culture, but that also promoted
the idea of consensus and consolidation. In the latter count, Maria
Vardoulakis's *Gold in the Streets* (1945) functioned similarly.
Judging by the circumstances of the book's publication, its author

---

[9]Robert Gorham Davis, "Invaded Selves." Review of *A Dream of Kings* by
Harry Mark Petrakis. *The Hudson Review* 19 (1966): 659-668.

[10]See Ted Morgan, "A Story Assigned by Fate." Review of *Eleni* by Nicholas
Gage, *New York Times Book Review* (May 1, 1983): 1, 18; William Henry,
"Mother's Love, Son's Revenge." *Time* (April 25, 1983): 113; C. M. Woodhouse,
"The Tragedy in Lia." *New York Review of Books* (August 18, 1983): 25-26.

was called forth to make up for an absence in the literature of the emerging Greek American community: to create an immigrant novel although she herself was not an immigrant. Her work was encouraged, published and awarded a prize, but its author never produced another novel and eventually disappeared completely. Her book, however, was to be remembered as the prototypical Greek American immigrant novel. Coming on the upsurge of Greek nationalistic pride during WW II and in the wake of Greece's successful resistance to the Axis powers, the book also came in a moment when the Greek American community and its middle class were in the process of consolidation. It elaborated several popular themes of immigration fiction and it affirmed and condoned assimilation as well as the virtues of the American Dream. If there was such a thing as the Greek American canon, we could say that Vardoulakis's novel was assigned to stand at its beginning overshadowing a more prolific writer such as Demetra Vaka-Brown on the basis of the more functionally correct, unambiguous and "modern" ideological choice it touted.

However cited her text might be, Maria Vardoulakis was considered an ethnic writer, meaning that her work was not deemed worthy of serious critical attention. She remained *the* Greek American writer whose work functioned as a "token" along with that of Harry Mark Petrakis in the compilation of ethnic literature anthologies. It is interesting to observe that Petrakis was branded an ethnic writer but denounced the title, sensing correctly the negative connotations it had. Also worthy of note is that Elia Kazan has not been considered ethnic or at least not to the extent Petrakis has, in spite of the fact that he has published several bestselling novels dealing semi-autobiographically with his immigrant/ethnic experience. Is the explanation that Kazan was an already accomplished mainstream artist and could not be discounted as a mere ethnic?

The problems for Greek American literature, nevertheless, are not minimized if we attempt to legitimize its canon drawing from the example of the pathbreaking work by ethnic scholars who try to shatter the silence surrounding the discussion of the ethnic factor in American literature. What are we to make, for example, of the fact that in Greek American literature we have no "authentic" immigrant writers who explore the immigration theme or who create a Greek American immigrant text?[11] Vaka-Brown gave us a personal narrative in *A Child of the Orient* (1914) well couched in the memories of her narrator's Oriental childhood and adulthood in Constantinople. Two short chapters in a book of 300 pages, however, is a rather poor representation for an ethnic group of 500,000. Despite the commonly held opinion to the contrary, there were proportionally many educated immigrant men and women who wrote primarily in Greek, even in the New World. Why is it that the immigration story did not appeal to them? Why did they publish poetry instead or short stories which focused either on the persistence of classical culture in modern Greece or on the nostalgic recollection of the motherland following the prevalent modes of Greek poets and prose writers living primarily under the heavy shadow of Palamas—the foremost Greek poet and the strongest proponent of demoticism at the turn of the century? It is not until we get to Theano Papazoglou-Margaris that we encounter an "authentic" Greek American immigrant writer. Even she publishes her stories rather late in a book form (first in the late 1930s and then again in the late 1950s and early 1960s).

An inevitable question is whether the immigration story constitutes an indispensible part for the canon of an ethnic literature, or is it a constructed paradigm meant to establish a developmental model for any ethnic literature and to inform critical thought with the idea of a literary "Darwinism"? In that case the past functions as the preparatory ground which prefigures the more significant present; in other words, the implication is that immigrant novels are artistically inferior in comparison with the work of the second generation.

However, if the immigration story is indeed a universal, what does its absence signify for Greek American literature? Is it perhaps a lack of a legitimate beginning both for the literature *and* for the community? Maria Vardoulakis provided the *first* immigrant novel in English; her book, nevertheless, is interesting not so much because it raises questions of "authenticity"—she was not an immigrant—but because its production is a state-

---

[11]Notice the problems that Torgovnick points out as far as Puzo's *The Godfather* is concerned. Marianna De Marco Torgovnick, "*The Godfather* as the World's Typical Novel," *South Atlantic Quarterly* 87 (Spring 1988): 329-353.

ment *about* the power of sociocultural forces that associate the foundation of a legitimate canon with the sociocultural legitimation of the community (Greek ethnic pride after WW II and the rise to the status of the middle class). Moreover, such a legitimation necessitated essentially the re-writing of Greek American literary history. It involved a "starting over" which decentered the early texts by Stephanini, Kazantzis, Vaka-Brown, Michalaros and others. It goes without saying that it was not coincidental that *Gold in the Streets* was a novel which promoted national consensus and consolidation.

Thus a structural paradigm involving the whole corpus of ethnic literature can prove inapplicable, but more importantly it can be falsifying and ideologically suspect. To attempt to discuss Greek American literature along the lines prescribed by other more often discussed ethnic texts is to attempt to give this less known literary canon a substance and a form, or to make it perform functions that do not normally obtain and therefore to forge a slanted "re-writing" of its "genealogy." It is another instance of "humanizing" the "other," a process that translates into alienating and marginalizing it even more.

It is a process that alienates and marginalizes by including. What is evident in Greek American literature today is a far more serious process of exclusion and delegitimation. We have already seen how language has functioned as a specious factor for the exclusion of certain texts. Another equally serious strategy of exclusion is the association of ethnic literature in general and Greek American in particular with sociological documentation. In other words, ethnic authenticity becomes a function of authenticating the ethnic presence in the New World. Hence critics and theorists determine *ethnic* themes and situations which exclusively relate ethnic literature to the American experience.[12] What is the position of obviously ethnic writers whose work does not fall within these parameters? Is their work to be excluded as not ethnically pertinent or to be included as a far more radical gesture of "difference"?

[12]The work of the following is paradigmatic of this tendency: William Boelhower, "The Immigrant Novel as Genre," *MELUS* 8 (Spring 1981): 3-13; Mary Dearborn, *Pocahontas's Daughters: Gender and Ethnicity in American Culture* (New York: Oxford University Press, 1986); Werner Sollors, *Beyond Ethnicity* (New York: Oxford University Press, 1986).

If ethnic literature is a literature of authentication how does one bring into the canon of Greek American literature the work of Byron Vazakas, Themistocles Hoetis, Evan Chigounis, and Olga Broumas? The literary fate of these writers is paradigmatic of what usually happens; they are either ignored completely as in the case of Hoetis and Chigounis, or their work is subsumed under a category other than the ethnic one. Vazakas has been associated and discussed within the modernistic movement and more particularly in his association with William Carlos Williams. Olga Broumas, on the other hand, has been brought into literary prominence for her important contribution to a feminist poetics and has often been discussed in connection with Adrienne Rich.[13]

On another level writers such as Stratis Haviaras, Kimon Lolos, and Irini Spanidou face an even more dire situation. Their work is considered neither Greek, nor American, nor Greek American. When published originally their work was enthusiastically received. Lolos's story "Mule No. 045" was even included among the *Best American Short Stories* of 1964; Haviaras's *When the Tree Sings* (1979) and Spanidou's *God's Snake* (1986) were nominated for National Book Awards for best first novels. However, since their publication these novels have been discussed neither as Greek—they were written originally in English—nor as American—their content deals exclusively with Greek subject-matter—nor as Greek American—they lack identifiable ethnic situations and themes. Hence these highly accomplished books have been relegated to critical neglect out of embarrassment. What paradigm can they be made to fit? How do they contribute to the development of our discussion of ethnic literature? These are the most commonly asked questions when one submits a paper on any of these writers to a journal that publishes and promotes articles on American ethnic writers. Naturally, such questions become powerful exclusion strategies which are entrenched in the ethnic scholar's embarrassment with the intractability of these texts. Thus a number of very important

[13]See, for example, Mary J. Carruthers, "The Revision of the Muse: Adrienne Rich, Audre Lorde, Judy Grahn, Olga Broumas," *The Hudson Review* 36 (Summer 1983): 292-322; Brian Bremen, "The Radiant Gist: The Poetry Hidden in the Prose of William's *Paterson*." *Twentieth Century Literature* 32 (Summer 1986): 221-241.

works are excluded from the Greek American canon. What chances then are there for a minor ethnic literature when some of its most powerful statements are denied access to the critical *mythos?*

In the light of what has been pointed out so far we can claim that the state of exclusion of Greek American literature is due both to the limiting canonizing attitudes of mainstream critics and the similar attitudes of some ethnic critics. We do not contend that the canonizing attitudes of the latter are meant to be exclusionary but rather that their choices and paradigm building are often inherently so.

The question remains though how to establish a valid Greek American canon avoiding the pitfalls already pointed out. I believe that we need to liberate our literary texts from serving functions largely dictated by what we have come to call mainstream canon but also by the "subsidiary" canon the mainstream one gives rise to in order to exorcise guilt and to create an image of the "other" compatible with and contained within the mainstream canon's image of itself.[14] In this sense I criticize any attempt which will be implemented to integrate mainstream and ethnic; in my opinion to integrate means to demote implicitly or even worse to marginalize.

As Henry Louis Gates Jr. aptly remarks, African American literature has been used for the longest time largely to prove the humanity of "our nig" rather than to be evaluated as a linguistic text along the lines that, say, Joyce's *Ulysses,* has been evaluated.[15] In the same way Greek American literature has been used to prove the humanity of that particular "other" by pointing out this "other's" quick assimilation and functioning according to Anglo-American prescriptions of conduct. To paraphrase Olga Broumas's poem, "Artemis":

> We are ethnics committed to
> a politics
> of transliteration, the methodology

---

[14]Barbara Hernstein Smith, "Contingencies of Value," *Critical Inquiry* 10 (September 1983): 18.
[15]Henry Louis Gates Jr., *Figures in Black* (New York and Oxford: Oxford University Press, 1987).

of a mind

stunned at the suddenly
possible shifts of meaning—for which
like amnesiacs

in a ward on fire, we must
find words
or burn.[16]

[16]Olga Broumas, *Beginning with O* (New Haven: Yale University Press, 1977): 24.

Rebetika in the United States
Before World War II

OLE L. SMITH

Once written off and stigmatized as music from the under-
world, associated with criminal activity among the lowest strata
of society, believed to be performed only in hash dens and prisons,
rebetika songs have since 1974 enjoyed a certain commercial
success in Greece, where reissues of the old recordings from the
1930s have been put out in great quantities. At the same time,
younger musicians have formed bands that try, not without
success, to play the older styles, popularizing songs otherwise
known only from rare and almost unplayable 78rpm records.[1] This
revival requires discussion in a much wider context than is possible here, but one aspect is important for the Greek American
cultural perspective: this upsurge of interest in older rebetika
has resulted in a number of rare American recordings of Greek
artists from the pre-World War II period becoming available
on LP reissues. Though many recordings still are accessible
only in private record collections, it is possible to discuss at
recordings—especially since the whole field of ethnic records in
the U.S. has become the subject of systematic study in recent years.[2]

Greek music in the U.S. does not seem to have received
much attention, and even rebetika in Greece have not yet been
studied in such detail as to be of much use for a discussion of

---

[1]On the ambiguous nature of the rebetika revival see Gail Holst-Warhaft's
perceptive and polemical remarks in *The Aegean Review* 5 (1988): 9-14.

[2]See the excellent volume, *Ethnic Records in America: A Neglected Heritage*,
American Folklife Center. Library of Congress, Washington, DC, 1982. Greek
material, however, is only dealt with incidentally.

the American developments.[3] Certain problems of a general nature can be pointed out, however, and areas for further research identified.

Gail Holst's *Road to Rembetiko* was the first attempt to draw attention to a much neglected area of Greek popular culture.[4] This pioneer work was, for a long time, the only accessible serious introduction to and treatment of rebetika. Written when original recordings were still hard to come by and factual information extremely scarce, it was clearly a labor of love, inspired by a deep feeling for the world of rebetika. The author had the privilege of having heard several important performers playing and singing well near their prime. Since it took up the subject virtually from scratch, Holst's book inevitably also contained some errors.

During the 1970s a lot of material appeared but serious research cannot be found until the publication of Stathis Gauntlett's *Rebetika* in 1985, unless we include the work by Stathis Damianakos, whose Κοινωνιολογία τοῦ ρεμπέτικου from 1976 had a certain impact in Greece but was based on highly questionable methodological principles.[5] In this period a revised and enlarged edition of Elias Petropoulos's *Anthology* and Tasos Schorelis's four volumes of rebetika texts were also published.[6]

From research done until now the following points are of special importance for the present discussion:

(1) A certified chronology of Greek rebetika recordings does not exist, but the following data seem almost certain; we do not have any Greek recordings before 1925; the first recordings in Greece with tradi-

---

[3]The best scholarly book on rebetika—in spite of some shortcomings—is Stathis Gauntlett's *Rebetika* (Carmina Graeciae Recentioris, Athens: Denise Harvey, 1985). See also his essay in *Byzantine and Modern Greek Studies* 8 (1982/83): 77-102.

[4]Published in Athens by Denise Harvey, 1975. A Greek translation with an appendix covering the Greek postwar debate on rebetika appeared in 1977 from the same publisher.

[5]I have dealt with Damianakos's theories in a paper to be published in *Journal of Modern Hellenism* 6.

[6]Both these works are highly selective and do not give an objective picture of the whole material, not to speak of their often lamented inaccuracy in the transcription of the texts. The Department of Modern Greek and Balkan Studies of the University of Copenhagen will shortly issue revised transcriptions of prewar rebetika on LP reissues.

tional bouzouki accompaniment were made in 1933; and the Metaxas dictatorship from 1936 put restrictions on the material recorded.[7]

(2) Recordings from Greece before 1933 are exclusively cafe *aman* music in more or less "Oriental" style.

(3) The words *rebetiko* and *rebetes* seem not attested in Greece before 1933.

(4) The existing anthologies of texts are completely unreliable.

(5) The overwhelming majority of rebetika recordings have almost no published discographical information.

I emphasize these points because in the literature and in the sleeve notes to the reissues one is confronted with a great deal of misleading information. In Petropoulos's and Schorelis's anthologies one can find mentioned recordings dated from 1910-1920 with no evidence at all, to note but one type of misinformation. Gross errors are found in the transcriptions of texts even in the late 1980s.

We can now take a look at the American recordings of rebetika. I should perhaps stress that I will deal with recordings only, since our knowledge of live performances of Greek music in the United States before World War II is extremely limited, and in any case it is the documentary evidence supplied by the existing records that alone will allow a tolerably certified analysis. As far as I know no one has ever attempted to deal with Greek music in the U.S., and existing literature does not even mention the subject, apart from sparse references to Greek American performers of classical European music.

Though ethnic recordings started very early in the United States, the first rebetika/cafe *aman* music was not recorded until 1917.[8] It is not known why the record companies were so slow in realizing that there was a market for Greek music, but soon Greek recordings were issued in a quantity well above the average for ethnic material. It is instructive to notice that the

[7]Apart from a short period in 1946 the censorship introduced by Metaxas continued after the war until it was abrogated by PA.SO.K.

[8]See Richard Spottswood in *Ethnic Recordings* 51ff and in his liner notes to the LP "The Greek Popular Song in America."

1940 census shows the Greek Americans to be the 13th largest market, but the most active company, Columbia, has Greek records as the 5th largest group of ethnic material issued. Until 1940 well over 1,000 records were issued with Greek material by the main companies: Columbia, Victor, Decca and Okeh/ Odeon.[9] To this number must be added the still unknown quantity of titles on independent ethnic labels such as Panellinion, Orthophone, Balkan, etc. Of course not all of these were rebetika recordings, and in any case much more detailed research should be done on these and related problems. As far as I know we have no information about the actual sales of Greek recordings.

In order to judge what kind of material was recorded and why it was issued the following circular from Columbia to record dealers is useful:

> The 35 million foreigners making their home here are keenly on the alert for anything and everything which will keep alive the memories of their fatherland. . . . Their own home music played or sung by artists whose names are household words in their homelands—these they must have. They are patriotic, these foreigners, and their own intense interest in their own native music is strengthened by their desire that their children, brought or born in this new country shall share their love of the old.[10]

Thus, it would seem that the companies went after traditional Greek music, though of course it should be pointed out that unless they employed Greek A & R men, they were probably not always in a position to know whether they got what they wanted. Even so, from what has become generally available on reissues, it would seem that most of the material recorded is, in fact, traditional music without any awareness of or reference to the new situation of the immigrant. There are, however, exceptions that show how the Greek singers and musicians reacted to their new situation by taking up songs reflecting their American life and by being influenced from other folk music styles.

[9]Pekka Gronow in *Ethnic Recordings* 23.
[10]Columbia 1914 circular quoted from Spottswood, op. cit., 55.

In Markos Melton's song "Σακραμέντο Μπόστον" we
have a strictly traditional rebetika structure and melodic line with
a text that from its very title reveals that it is not a song from
"the distant fatherland." It is clearly based on American experience and shows American linguistic innovations:

Σακραμέντο καὶ Λοντάϊ
ὁ Θεὸς νὰ σὲ φυλάει.

Πέρασα κι' ἀπὸ τὸ Φρίσκο
ὅλο μπελαλῆδες βρίσκω.

Καὶ γραμμὴ στὸ Μπόστον πάω
γιατὶ πολὺ τ' ἀγαπάω.

Βρίσκω ὅλο μερακλῆδες,
χουβαρδάδες ζεϊμπεκλῆδες.

Μέσ' στὴ Νέα Ὑόρκη μπῆκα
ὅλο τζογαδόρους βρῆκα.

Πῆγα γιὰ νὰ πάρω τσέντζι
κι' ἔφυγα μὲ χωρὶς σένσι.[11]

On other recordings the American influence is even stronger,
and the music no longer seems particularly Greek. Yorgos
Katsaros's song "Μὲ τὶς τσέπες ἀδειανὲς" is far removed
from Greece, although it has been included on a reissue LP of
"traditional rebetika songs from the United States."[12]

Τί θὰ κάνουμε, ρὲ φίλοι,
στὴ κατάσταση αὐτή,
ποὺ χαμένοι πᾶμε ὅλοι
ἐδῶ στὴν Ἀμερική.

Ὅπου φτώχεια ἔχει πέσει
καὶ δὲν βρίσκουμε δουλειὰ

---

[11]Transcribed from the Falireas Bros. LP of Markos Melkon.
[12]It can also be found on the Falireas Bros. 2-LP set by Katsaros, where it
now is characterized as a "revue" song.

καὶ τὰ ἔξοδα δὲν βγαίνουν
καὶ τραβοῦμε συμφορά.

Πῶς θυμᾶμαι τὶς ἡμέρες
ποὺ 'χαμε τὰ τάλληρα,
ποὺ τρώγαμε μπριτζόλες,
καὶ τώρα τρῶμε λάχανα.

Ποὺ πηγαίναμε στοὺς γάμους,
καὶ φωνάζαμε ταξί,
τώρα πᾶμε μὲ τὰ πόδια,
μ' ἔξω εἰς τὴν ἐξοχή.

Ποὺ πηγαίναμε στὸ θέατρο,
καὶ φωνάζαμε ταξί,
τώρα πᾶμε μὲ τὰ πόδια
μ' ἔξω εἰς τὴν ἐξοχή.

Μὲ τὰ μοῦτρα κρεμασμένα,
μὲ τὶς τσέπες ἀδειανές,
περπατοῦμε μέσ' στοὺς δρόμους
μὰ μὲ σκέψεις, συλλογές.

Μὲ τὰ μοῦτρα κρεμασμένα,
μὲ τὶς τσέπες ἀδειανές,
περπατοῦμε μέσ' στοὺς δρόμους,
Χοῦβερ, τί μᾶς ἔκανες;

This song is a purely American product in text and music. It reflects the Depression experience, and there are no particular Greek values or norms in the song. It would probably be difficult to understand for Greeks living in Greece. We see here on a small scale the adaptation to American standards, values and culture. There are other examples, and a much more complete knowledge is required before we can work out the detailed development from purely Greek traditional music and song to hybrid forms and finally completely Americanized material.

A number of these U.S. recordings were exported to Greece, although it is still impossible to give precise information. At least some cases of unmistakable influence from imported U.S. recordings show that we should pay attention to the problem of American influence and dependence. As pointed out before, rebetika with bouzouki accompaniment were not recorded in Greece until 1933, when Yiorgos Batis and Markos Vamvakaris were first admitted to a studio. I will not here go into a discussion of the reasons for this, but only point to the social stigma attached to bouzouki music. It is probable, however, that what triggered developments in Greece were the U.S. recordings of Jack Gregory (alias G. Halkias) from 1932 which created some stir when exported to Greece. The veteran bouzouki player Yiannis Papaioannou in his autobiography says that he had never heard anything similar, and Halkias's success obviously contributed to the decision of the Greek companies to record local bouzouki players. Nor should it be overlooked that the first examples of non-cafe *aman* rebetika recordings were made by the Greek American singer Dimitris Kostis (for the British Grammophone Co.) in Athens in 1930, three years before Markos's and Batis's first recordings in a similar style.[13]

The word *rebetiko* first occurs on American labels. This observation was originally made by Gauntlett,[14] who stated that the earliest (to judge from its catalog number) record to have the word *rebetiko* on its label is Marika Papaghika's Ντούρου-Ντούρου" on Col. 56113. The term *rebetiko* appears where the name of the dance usually is given. On the label of Yannakis Ioannidis's recording issued on Col. 56137 we find both *rebetiko* and *zeibekiko,* but the first term is translated "Greek Bum Song." It would thus seem that the term could be used both as a designation for the type of song and of the dance. But there is no such dance as "rebetiko." The term can only be taken as describing the type of song. The date of these recordings is not given, but from the matrix numbers allocated to Ioannidis's two titles that date seems to be approximately 1929. In Greece the word seems unattested before Bayanderas's recording of "Πάντα μὲ γλυκὸ χασίσι" which is some years later than 1933, and the first occurrence of ρεμπέτης is on Markos Vamvakaris's first

---

[13]See Gauntlett, *Rebetika* 212 and 223.
[14]Op. cit. 32 n. 185. See also his paper mentioned above n. 3, pp. 83ff.

recordings from 1933.[15] It would be strange if the musicians in
Athens took over a term used by their American colleagues,
though this is, in fact, what is suggested by the available evid-
ence. Gauntlett's chronology, however, is not wholly accurate;
I have found the word *rebetiko* as early as 1927 on a record by
G. Vidalis (Odeon K 28044) issued in the United States.

The need for more research to be done in this area of American influence on rebetika in Greece—not to mention more detailed investigation of the development of rebetika in the U.S.
as well as in Greece is clear. There is also a problem relating to
the reissue situation. Until now anthologies have been compiled
without any thought of systematic presentation. There is a very
good collection on the 2-LP set "The Greek Popular Song in
America" issued in Greece by the Falireas Bros. with more than
usually informative liner notes by Richard Spottswood. There is
no discographical information at all. The 5-LP set on Greek CBS
"Παραδοσιακὰ τραγούδια ἠχογραφημένα στὶς ΗΠΑ τὶς
πρῶτες δεκαετίες τοῦ αἰῶνα" is a bit of a misnomer for
chronological reasons and because some of the songs are from
Katsaros's most non-traditional repertoire. For reasons of copyright, presumably, these LPs are also without discographical
notes. An older collection edited by Tasos Schorelis on Greek
CBS "Τὰ πρῶτα ρεμπέτικα 1901-1913" contains great material although the album title is based on Schorelis's fantastic
error of taking the copyright dates on the labels as the recording
dates. Some further LPs produced by the Falireas Bros. under the
title "Τὸ ρεμπέτικο τραγούδι στὴν 'Αμερικὴ" contain both
U.S. and Greek material, and it is a bit of a mystery why this
title has been chosen. The same pertains to a collection of songs
about TB. Recently a 2-LP set by Katsaros and an LP by Markos
Melkon have added to available documentation, but it is surely
time for a scholarly researched reissue program. Richard
Spottswood's forthcoming discographical work may make it possible to get a basis for such a project.

In our present context, however, we should not overlook the
evidence of the rebetika recordings and the light they throw on
both cultural continuity and on the process of cultural assimilation
and adaptation of the Greek immigrants: the way in which the

[15]Text printed in Gauntlett, op. cit., as No. C34.

traditional medium of rebetika is used both to keep alive traditional culture and to convey new experience and perceptions to a point where the traditional medium breaks down and gives way to a not specifically ethnic medium. It is clearly time that rebetika take their rightful place among the other performing arts, to give a truer and more complex picture of the Greek American experience. The American material also shows the possibilities of a medium that was never really explored and developed. This problem, however, cannot be solved in isolation from the wider scene of American popular music.[16]

[16]I would like to thank Gail Holst-Warhaft for her valuable help on a number of points and Helen Papanikolas for bringing to my notice a catalog of Greek records from 1927-1928.

Greek and Romanian Immigrants As Hyphenated Americans: Toward a Theory of White Ethnicity

G. JAMES PATTERSON

Research on Romanians and Greeks in North America suggests some generalizations about white ethnicity which can be offered as theoretical postulates. They are as follows:

(1) White ethnics (Romanians, Greeks, Serbians and so forth) may be termed "hyphenated North Americans" since they retain their ethnic identity while also being American or Canadian. In many parts of the world, ethnic groups constitute a discrete and separate category; affiliation with an ethnic group is ascriptive. In North America one may move in and out of white ethnic identification as desired. The non-ascriptive character of white ethnicity in North America allows for a great deal of situational ethnicity. It is usually voluntary, functional and pragmatic.[1] Most Romanians and Greeks in North America use ethnic institutions for help with adaptation to the new culture, and later move in and out of ethnic church, club and even kinship ties as their own personal needs and socio-economic aspirations dictate.

[1]More information on Romanians in North America can be found in my work, *The Romanians of Saskatchewan: Four Generations of Adaptation* (Ottawa: National Museum of Man, 1977) and in my "The Persistence of White Ethnicity in Canada: The Case of the Romanians," *East European Quarterly* 19 (1985): 493-500, from which certain passages and information in this section are taken.

(2) Ethnic neighborhoods are disappearing, and family and voluntary associations, especially the homeland church, are primary centers of ethnic affiliation and identity. There are exceptions to the above, to be sure; most white ethnic neighborhoods in North America are losing their character and disappearing.

There is not much left of Chicago's Greek Town on Halstead Street. The last *kafeneion* in Denver closed in 1970. Small but flourishing Greek communities in the western mining towns of Pueblo and Trinidad, Colorado, described so well by Zeese Papanikolas[2] are gone, as they are in Price and Helper, Utah, as described by Helen Papanikolas.[3] The Greek Town of Portland, Oregon, illustrated in a book of photographs by Thomas Doulis[4] is a thing of the past, as is the Tacoma, Washington, community studied by Robert Theodoratus.[5] The churches remain, but the residential neighborhoods are gone. The Canadian cities of Vancouver and Toronto are exceptions, due to immigration policies in Canada different from those in the U.S., and more arrivals of new immigrants, but even these communities are becoming North Americanized and diluted as their members move into prosperity and dispersion.

(3) Assimilation, syncretism and cultural maintenance are three different white ethnic adaptations to the North American setting. Many of the third and fourth generations are assimilating and losing their ethnic identity. Others, through syncretism, are developing a "Third Culture," which is an amalgam of homeland and North American influences. Cultural maintenance is perpetuated by "core ethnics."[6]

[2]Census of Canada (Ottawa, Statistics Canada, 1981).

[3]Gerald J. Bobango, *The Romanian Orthodox Episcopate of America: The First Half Century* (Jackson, Michigan: Romanian-American Heritage Center, 1979).

[4]For more information, see my "The "Unassimilated Greeks of Denver," *Anthropological Quarterly* 4 (1970): 243-253.

[5]G. James Patterson, *The Greeks of Vancouver: A Study in the Preservation of Ethnicity* (Ottawa: National Museum of Man, 1976).

[6]M. Elaine Burgess, "The Resurgence of Ethnicity: Myth or Reality?" *Ethnic and Racial Studies* 1 (1978): 265-285.

For those choosing to keep their Romanian and Greek identities, cultural syncretism frequently has occurred. English words are inserted into Romanian or Greek. Homeland music, food, folklore and other customs are Americanized. A "Third Culture," neither fully Romanian nor Greek nor North American, has emerged. This adaptation sometimes emphasizes stereotypes of the homeland as held by the new culture, and often distorts and even caricatures what it is trying to emulate. The dilution of the homeland culture varies based on the number of new immigrants, the frequency of contact members have with the homeland and the intensity of that contact, and other factors.

Many Romanian and Greek North American rites of passage, folk dancing, holiday celebrations and homeland food consumption have become a created tradition, more symbolic than all-encompassing.[7] But the fact is that ethnic activities continue, even in altered or diluted form.

For centuries the Orthodox Church has assumed the role of guardian and perpetuator of the culture in alien or hostile environments; the Church has played that role in the New World also. Working through the Church are the "core ethnics," those who choose to retain and emphasize their ethnic heritage. Simic offers a useful analysis of the activities of Serbian American retirees who return to the bosom of Serbian ethnicity after successfully pursuing careers and lives apart from the homeland groups. These are people who found it economically feasible to pursue careers in the North American mainstream. Few rejected the homeland Church and culture, but they were not deeply involved in it during their most productive years. Other core ethnics are recent immigrants and those who gain emotional and religious sustenance from their ethnic ties.[8]

Romanian-North American and Greek-North American ethnicity can be seen as a model for viewing other white ethnic groups. The theoretical approaches presented, which include a view of ethnicity as non-ascriptive, neighborhoods as disappearing with the Church as the guardian of the language and culture,

[7]Zeese Papanikolas, *Buried Unsung: Louis Tikas and the Ludlow Massacre* (Salt Lake City: University of Utah Press, 1982).

[8]Helen Papanikolas, "The Greeks of Carbon County," *Utah Historical Quarterly* 22 (1954): 143-164. See also *Emilia-Emily; Yoryis-George* (Salt Lake City: University of Utah Press, 1987).

and various types of white ethnic adaptation to the North American setting, could be used in studying other immigrant groups from Europe.

Some ten years ago I suggested in print that white ethnicity in America was overstated and exaggerated.[9] While my most recent data on Romanians and Greeks show high levels of assimilation, they also show a dogged persistence of homeland cultural elements, at least among core ethnics and new arrivals. Use of the approaches outlined in this paper could be applied to other similar groups on this continent and perhaps elsewhere. Immigration history and the ethnography of white ethnic groups in North America, as studied by anthropologists, is a field largely devoid of theory. Without theory we will only have the descriptive community studies a number of us have produced. With a theory we might come to understand the meaning of white ethnicity, and why it continues to persist when much suggests that it should not.

Appendix A—Romanians

The early Romanians can be divided into two groups. The first were mostly Bukovinian peasants who homesteaded in Saskatchewan and Alberta at the turn of the century. The second was centered in the industrial heartland of the U.S. Great Lakes states, especially in Cleveland, Detroit, and Chicago.[10] Post-World War II immigrants from Romania have settled in Ontario, founding communities in Windsor, Kitchener, Hamilton, and Toronto, and in Montreal, Quebec. There are at present about 22,000 ethnic Romanians in Canada[11] and 65,000 in the U.S.[12] Almost all of the immigrants were unskilled laborers. Those settling on the Canadian prairies became farmers, while those in the cities became factory workers.

[9]Thomas Doulis, *A Surge to the Sea: The Greeks in Oregon* (Portland, Oregon: Lockie and Associates, 1977).

[10]Robert J. Theodoratus, *A Greek Community in America: Tacoma, Washington* (Sacramento, California: The Sacramento Anthropological Society, 1971).

[11]Andrei Simic, "Ethnicity as a Career for the Elderly: The Serbian American Case," *The Journal of Applied Gedontology* 6 (1979): 112-126.

[12]See Herbert J. Gans, "Symbolic Ethnicity: The Future of Ethnic Groups and Cultures in America." *Ethnic and Racial Studies* 2 (1979): 1-20.

The common pattern was for male emigration, often with the intent of staying in the New World for a few years, making a nest egg or fortune, and returning home with the money. *Mia si drumul,* "a thousand dollars and back home," was the phrase describing the expectations of many of the early immigrants. While many in fact did return, others stayed, establishing churches and communities.

The first Romanian Orthodox church in North America was St. Nicholas, in Regina, Saskatchewan, founded in 1902. There were some eleven Romanian Orthodox churches and communities founded during this decade in Saskatchewan and Alberta, as well as several Romanian Jewish homestead colonies. Today the primary Romanian communities in Western Canada are in Regina and Edmonton.

The Cleveland, Detroit, and Chicago communities were the most important in the U.S. Here the immigrant experience was urban and industrial. Romanian neighborhoods developed, centering around an Orthodox church. Mutual aid societies, insurance companies, grocery stores, bakeries, candy stores, bars and other establishments catered to the immigrants. After World War II the old ethnic neighborhoods began to decline, and as residents moved to the suburbs, the churches followed.

Postwar settlements in Ontario and Montreal are comprised of better educated immigrants than were characteristic of the original communities. These Romanian-Canadian neighborhoods continue to receive new influxes of immigrants from Romania, many of them professional people who are political refugees.

Appendix B—Greeks of Denver and Vancouver

Rather than summarize the history of Greek settlements in North America, as I have just done for the Romanians, I shall focus instead on two communities I have studied in depth: Denver, Colorado, and Vancouver, British Columbia.

The Denver Greeks arrived at the turn of the century, having originally been attracted by work in the mines and on the railroad. Some came by a process of chain migration, some as indentured workers, and some were hired in New York by labor recruiters. They worked at a variety of jobs, often graduating from a push-cart venture to a candy store, coffee house or restaurant. One pattern is clear: as soon as the laborer or employee was able to go into business for himself or in some way free himself from having to work for someone else, he did so. The Greek pattern of placing a premium on personal independence seems to be one of the factors causing this.

As the early male immigrants began to prosper, they sent home for wives, and established churches. In Denver the Hellenic Orthodox Church was founded in 1906. Near the church an ethnic neighborhood developed. In the 1920s the Denver Greek Town had five restaurants serving mainly Greek food and some fourteen coffee houses.

As the members of the community prospered, a classic demographic change took place. The original Greek Town was located downtown. By the 1920s Greek residents had moved about a mile southeast of the city center; a new church was founded there in 1933. After World War II yet another church was built some six miles southeast of the downtown by second- and third-generation descendants of immigrants who had begun to become assimilated and had reached solidly middle class status. This church and community center serves as the locus of the religious and social life of the Greeks of Denver today.

Only a Greek grocery store, a Greek-owned restaurant and homeland-style *kafeneion* were left in the original Greek Town when I did field work there in the 1960s. In the early 1970s the entire area was razed by a "Model Cities" urban renewal project. The eighty or so unassimilated old men whose lives centered around the *kafeneion* were dispersed; all have since died. Today Denver's Greek Town is gone; in its place are parking lots and high-rise office buildings.[13]

Vancouver, British Columbia, had a small prewar Greek community in the East End which later moved to the Kitsilano region with the establishment of a church in the 1930s. Restrictive U.S. immigration policies and the attractiveness of Vancouver to Greeks were factors in the rapid expansion of the Vancouver community after World War II. Today there are over 6,000 Greeks in the Kitsilano section of Vancouver and at least 10,000

[13]Simic, *ibid.*

in the metropolitan area. Continuing immigration by Greeks to Vancouver in large numbers has assured the continuance of a myriad of Greek businesses, social service agencies, community center, restaurants, coffee houses, and, of course, the Church.[14]

Appendix C—Degree and Nature of Assimilation

Inevitably, in discussing immigration patterns which began several generations ago, the question of assimilation must be addressed. I find it useful to measure assimilation among white ethnics in North America using two primary criteria: exogamy and loss of language. Using these criteria, most of the Romanians, except those in the newest settlements in Eastern Canada, are largely assimilated. In Western Canada in particular, only about six percent of Romanians speak the language at home. In the cities, Romanian churches and clubs continue to exist, but most of the rural wooden Byzantine-style Romanian Orthodox churches are closed, used only occasionally or not at all, empty reminders of a once-flourishing Balkan culture on the prairies.

The Montreal and Ontario communities possess an exogamy and language-loss rate of about 50 percent, but continue to receive new infusions of homeland culture with each new immigrant. However, since many of these people are refugees, glad to be gone from an economic and political system they dislike, the more successful of them tend to shed homeland cultural baggage quickly.

Greeks, too, are tending to assimilate in Denver and Vancouver, but less than Romanians. The Greek Diaspora is a well-documented phenomenon; its ideal final phase is returning to the homeland, and when this happens, cultural connections between the homeland and the host country continue. I would hardly suggest the early Romanian immigrants missed their homeland any less than did the Greeks, but my interviews with old-timers of both cultures for the past two decades suggest more verbalization of nostalgia for the mother country among Greeks, more return visits, and more travel back and forth between Greece

[14]G. James Patterson, "A Critique of 'The New Ethnicity.'" *American Anthropologist* 81 (1979): 103-105.

and North America than between Romania and North America. The Romanian estrangement from the homeland is exacerbated by politics; postwar Romanian refugees are extremely grateful for whatever opportunities they gain in North America, are relieved to escape a totalitarian state, and have greater difficulty returning than do Greeks. I do not have estimates for the rates of exogamy and loss of language among contemporary Greek communities in North America, though I would estimate that both exceed 50 percent for Denver and a little less for Vancouver.

Arranged Marriage in Greek America: The Modern Picture Bride

CONSTANCE CALLINICOS

The following paper is based on 300 interviews done with Greek American women born and raised in 20 states, both in rural and urban areas. Their parents were first-wave immigants from all areas of Greece (and Asia Minor) of the 1920s and 1930s. The interviews were conducted with first-, second-, third-, and fourth-generation women from 1976 to 1989. Ane hundred and ten were made in preparation for my book American Aphrodite *(New York: Pella, 1990).*

In my interviews with second- and third-generation women, inevitably, almost unavoidably, the subject of the arranged marriage and what it meant to us as Good Greek Girls would be discussed in detail. How could we not discuss it? The very fact of being *Good Greek Girls* means knowing about arranged marriages, and having definite opinions about them. We cannot talk about our lives without talking about this aspect of becoming female among our people, and its connection to how we view life.

Indeed, many of us learned firsthand about it on our first trip to Greece. I know that is how I first experienced *proxenia.* My well-meaning Athenian uncle (my father's older brother) proposed to me and to my mother (I was 16 at the time) that certain upper-class young men and their fathers had been making discreet inquiries regarding his well-off American relatives. It was known that they had daughters, and could a deal be struck for a merger? [Marriage . . .] Of course my mother asked me about this. Of course I refused. We laughed about it. And that was the end of that. But it stuck with me, as it did with so many of the women I talked to. I recall being asked when I later returned to my senior year in high school about the highlights of my trip to Greece, and relating, first above all other experiences, this innocuous tale. My response: NO ARRANGED MARRIAGE. NO PROXENIA. NOT EVER.

The arranged marriage is alive and well in Greek America. And no, not just among the newly arrived in the ghetto enclaves such as Astoria. In California: San Francisco, Ventura County, Los Angeles. In Chicago. In small towns in Michigan and Indiana. In Massachusetts. In New Hampshire. In Washington, D.C. Wherever Greek Americans are gathered and live, arranged marriages continue to occur. I know of them personally. And I have been told of them by women, both young and old, who will come up to me after I have presented a paper, or have spoken of this topic at a Greek gathering.

I have been told about them by young men (and not-so-young men), American-born as well as Greek-born, who have been approached with propositions for these "deals" and are repelled by such practices. An academic from the Midwest related that he was told after he tried to clarify to the matchmaker his views on romantic love and sexual compatibility: what difference does it make if you know her or not? They all look the same under the covers, anyway.

I have heard about these marriages from fathers who have been approached for their daughters, both Greek-born and American-born. All of this has occurred within the last two years. Again, from my own experience with this phenomenon, I heard about arranged marriage from my husband. Shortly after we became engaged in the early 70s, my fiance, a Greek American man (one of the most non-"Greek" types one could meet in those days), related a story like this to me as if it were a joke (at least *he* thought it was amusing).

He described to me his father's disappointment and anger that his son was forging ahead with a valueless marriage to a woman he had "fallen in love with" (his father sneered those words when he said them). How on earth, he lamented, could his son be such a dolt? Why would he not accept a deal that he had spent months negotiating with a *patrioti* who offered apartment buildings in Manhattan? The woman offered as part of this package was a beautiful woman (about 19 or 20 at the time) about 15 years younger than my fiance and, as described by his father, "ripe." Indeed. "Ripe." Like plums. Or apricots. Or apples. Ready for consumption.

Arranged marriage today is not the same in practice as it was during the time of my *Yaya*. The *prika* (dowry) is different. Rather than the folksy hand-embroidered offerings, copper kettles and *candiles* of our village grandmothers, and a share in the *ktimata* or *stremata* (parcels of family land) from the home village, considerable amounts of cash and condos, partnerships in business, and real estate holdings are offered to enhance the offering of one man to another man of his greatest burden and liability, his daughter.

The modern picture bride wears designer clothes. She is adorned with jewelry, fine gold, pearl and diamond adornments. Schooled in high-fashion *coiffure* and *maquillage,* she presents herself to a potential *gambro* (bridegroom) as a proud showpiece of her father's financial success. She may have been presented at one of the many imitation-Anglo "cotillion" Debutante Balls that are the fashion among affluent Greek Americans. These balls continue "tradition" by enlisting a former debutante (now a flagship member of the more affluent church community Ladies' Philoptochos Society) to teach "the girls" how to walk and "move." The "girls" also receive training in what gowns are appropriate, how to hold a bouquet of fresh flowers, how to smile, and where to point a nose when curtsying.

To be sure, she is educated. But not too educated. Her education is more the finishing-school variety. Cosmetic. Perhaps a teaching degree. Elementary Ed is safe enough, and likely to be looked upon with favor as not too "uppity" or threatening to the ego of a potential son-in-law. Greatly discouraged is scholarly pursuit (which would render her unfit for *nikokirio* or motherhood, or church work), or any profession geared to giving priority to a life work or direct contributions to society. A 28-year-old woman I interviewed tells me she still hears from her mother that "college" where she earned a Master's Degree in Chemical Engineering "ruined" her. Likewise her involvement in sports, which her parents believed made her look, walk and act too much like a man. Muscle and a carefree stride just wouldn't do for the young woman preparing for Greek marriage.

The groom or "gambro" is college-educated, most preferably a lawyer, doctor or business/finance major. Professors will do, but they don't make a lot of money, and they're not very interested in business.

One of the more barbaric aspects of this process, the presentation of a bloody sheet as proof of virginity, has gone by the wayside. However, this does not minimize virginity as one of the key prizes in these marriages. It only means that in modern Greek America, men will not come to blows and families will not sue in civil court if the bride has not convincingly bled on her wedding night. I have interviewed Greek-American women as old as 48 who still zealously guard their virginity for the coming of the Greek Prince, who seems never to materialize.

Such a delicate subject is no longer considered good form to publicly debate. The men in question will talk about it. Apologies will be exchanged. In many cases, as documented by Constantina Safilios-Rothschild[1] and feminists in Greece, the bride and her mother will have "taken care" of the problem before marriage by surgical restoration of virginity, a simple procedure of stitching up the offending woman so that she will be guaranteed to bleed, thus causing no embarassment and shame to Papa and Mama. Until very recent years, surgical restoration of virginity was second only to illegal abortion as a moneymaker for doctors among Greeks both here and in the mother country:

> All brides were, naturally, virgins. If the sacrificial wedding night did not bring forth the ritual flow of blood, and if one's lord and master was not satisfied by the color and quantity, the disgraced female would be sent back to her father's house with blows on her back and the seal of shame on her and her family forever. This did not happen only in rural hamlets.

[1]Constantina Safilios-Rothschild, Chrysie Constantelos, and Basil B. Karadaras, "The Greek-American Woman" (Paper presented at *The Greek Experience In America,* Symposium 1976). University of Chicago: 1976.

I knew girls personally who had rushed within hours of their marriage to be sewn back up into respectability with a dab of dove's blood by certain doctors who plied that trade. My own aunt, marrying for the first time at the age of 47, was one of their customers.[2]

The wedding, however, after all analysis, is only a ritual. Marriage as a choice in and of itself does not hold negative meaning for any of us. What is negative is the socialization process that culminates in the subservient and passive personality of the Good Greek Girl who calmly assents to the transaction of arranged marriage, having been raised by her Good Greek Parents to believe that Papa knows best how to take care of her, and that he can be trusted to choose the correct lifemate, as he should be trusted to choose the correct life for us.

Despite the new version of *prika,* the meaning of these transactions remains unchanged. The issues are control, ownership and kinship. As Gayle Rubin has documented in *Toward An Anthropology of Women,* men become kin to one another by the exchange of property and women as chattel. Rubin called it "The Traffic in Women."[3] If a male has a daughter and she becomes another's wife, they become kinsmen. The daughter is just another possession like the goods exchanged with her: cattle, land, household goods, etc.

As recently as 1978, a young American-born woman of 20 was given in arranged marriage by her parents to a husband 25 years her senior. She was to live in Greece with him. She was a picture bride, never having met her husband-to-be until a few weeks before the wedding in Greece, at which time the engagement occurred. She came to her future home (built and paid for by her father) with a made-in-America dowry, 1970s style: washing machine and dryer, American-French Provincial furniture, towels, sheets, china, crystal, an entire household shipped to Greece so that she might duplicate her American-style home there.[4]

[2]Lili Bita, "No Masters But Ourselves." *The Miami Herald,* February 20, 1983.

[3]Gayle Rubin, "The Traffic In Women," in: *Toward An Anthropology of Women,* Rayna B. Reiter, ed. (New York: Monthly Review Press, 1975).

[4]Constance Callinicos, *American Aphrodite.* New York: Pella, 1990. This

Other arranged marriages are the reverse. The male is the "picture groom." Arrangements are made across the Atlantic for him to emigrate to the United States. A dowry is offered. His ticket is paid for, and perhaps his education, if that is necessary.

As a feminist I am repelled by the notion that this sort of thing should be going on among my own people. I am personally offended by the thought that a woman's most important life decision next to her choice of career and profession should be taken out of her control and reduced to a set of negotiations in which she takes no active part except to nod her head yea or nay after the fact; indeed, reduced to a bargaining process in which her father's property and his wealth and success are the deciding factors in the choice of her lifemate (and, I might add, her lifelong bed partner).

I am also offended as a member of an ethnic group that is lately publicized as one of the two or three most successful, most affluent, most educated and assimilated populations in the U.S. The positive statistics regarding "struggle and success" as Charles Moskos describes our history in his book, *Greek Americans: Struggle and Success,* are woefully skewered in the wrong extreme for our women. We struggled, but we have not necessarily succeeded. I recoil from that kind of boosterism. I know that because of the built-in male bias of this self-congratulation, and because of our women's willing silence, most of the *xeni* (Greek Americans still refer to the rest of America as "foreigners" or *xeni*) outside of the Greek community have no idea what our lives are like. Beyond their contact with us as members of the Baklava Brigade, the smiling purveyors of Greek ethnicity found at the annual church festivals, they are ignorant, for the most part, of how we live and what we think.

I am disappointed at the response I must offer to the question asked of me by a non-Greek American sociology professional in New York: "How could a young woman be born and raised here in the U.S., go to high school here, graduate, and then consent to an arranged marriage with a guy she doesn't know?" My answer must always be "that doesn't surprise me." Her preparation for tacit consent begins in the cradle. According to a study of Greeks by Dr. Kiki Vlachouli Roe of UCLA,

3-month-old male infants are picked up more when they cry, they are cooed to in a decidely warmer tone than are female infants, they are talked to more, and in general treated much more specially by their mothers than are their baby sisters.[5]

What became most surprising to me, as I stacked up tape after tape of interviews, was this: how could a Greek woman hang in there (as so many did), against all odds, fighting every inch of her way with her brother, her father, her mother, and her church, and be sturdy enough to escape? How could she have the courage to say no, over and over, to parents and community who pose only the marriage option to her? How, in the face of the kind of pressure Good Greek Girls are up against, could she maintain the energy and presence of mind to persevere toward whatever educational and career goals she might have set for herself? Particularly if these goals conflict with her community's image of the "Real Greek Woman," when her very identity as a woman of her people is threatened and when she is presented with no alternatives to such a narrow definition of "female"?

With incredible difficulty. I might add that many simply burned out from frustration and gave up midstream. Many had incomplete college programs. Meaningless clerical jobs filled in time until they did the right Greek thing: got married. After all, better to marry the nice Greek Boy than have to fight so hard and long for the simple right to be left alone to get an education and have a life of one's own. Almost every woman I talked to who earned a college degree of any kind said she did so under duress. More parental pressure and emotional upheaval were reported by those who chose to pursue "non-domestic" degrees such as law, science, or engineering, rather than a field like teaching, which was "more harmonious with Greek family life."

One had a choice I was told (and these are one of my women's words) between "scratching, fighting, and kicking" for

material is taken from an interview which provided the basis for Chapter Two, "An Arranged Wedding in Greece: 1978."

[5]Kiki Vlachouli Roe, "Sex Differences in the Treatment of Three-Month-Old Greek Infants As a Function of Differential Maternal Treatment" (Paper presented at *Yiorti: A Celebration of Greek Womanhood*, Symposium 1988). University of California at Los Angeles 1988.

the education she really wanted or leaving home and getting it for herself—Papa would not pay for professional degrees—or knuckling under and settling for living at home and going to teacher's college.

I suppose even with all these terrible stories told to me, I would be content to have documented our history, and proud of our present if I had found in my recent interviews with younger women in their twenties and early thirties that we'd come a long way. One can be tolerant, even forgiving, of first-generation immigrant parents who spoke little English, who feared the outsider's world and adhered to a system of socialization imported from the old country, not just for little girls but also for little boys. These days, it would be supposed, Greek Americans were doing better by their female children.

Not so. As of the 1970 census, approximately 85 percent of our men had earned college degrees. In comparison, only 20 percent of our women had attended college, and only half of those had completed it. More than half of Greek American men had earned advanced degrees. Of Greek American women, a miniscule minority had chosen graduate degrees in other subjects besides education or had ventured into the professional worlds of law and medicine.[6] It would seem that education for the American woman of Greek descent had not progressed, and was not as highly valued as it was for the American man of Greek descent.

I spoke to a woman who came from the Northeast, not far from where Mike Dukakis grew up. Her father was one of the minority of educated immigrant men, quite well off financially. He was, in fact, one of the first Greek Americans to earn a law degree. He had a son as well as a daughter. This woman's brother graduated from Harvard Law School. She was forced into a two-hour one-way commute to a teacher's college. When she asked her father why she couldn't be a lawyer, too, he replied, "You can be the legal secretary in my office, and we'll see," which she did for seven long years of what she called "indentured servitude" while waiting for her father to consent to her enrollment in law school. She claims to this day

[6]Alice Scourby, *The Greek Americans.* (Boston, Massachusetts: Twayne Publishers, 1984.)

that she learned more in her father's law office about the law than in three years of law school. In addition to her duties as indentured servant, she cooked, cleaned, ironed, gardened and kept the household going for the two men and her ill mother.

Her father never did consent. Thus, after nursing her mother through cancer and burying her, she left home to enter law school on her own. She cited the fading away of her brilliant mother's "wasted life" as the major impetus for her odyssey away from home. Her father was incensed that she would do such a thing. He did not speak to her for two years.

Curiously, however, when she had obtained her law degree, and had been working for a few years, he requested her return to the family circle as an attorney in his and her brother's law office. "No way," she told me she replied to him, and here her voice became the angriest it had been during the course of my three hours with her. "Not unless you sign a contract making me a partner." He refused. He persisted for years in insisting on his own terms before finally relenting and signing her contract. She described it as a major triumph in her life.

I have recorded stories told about teenage years of great conflict and sometimes violence in the lives of Greek American women. The disputes revolved around career choices, merely obtaining an education, and sexual freedom.[7] The details of arguments and shouting matches with one or both parents are familiar, as are the sneaking around to meet the kids down the block and the cover stories for dating the boys at school cooked up with Greek friends who were willing to help (even a brother might assist). I found pent-up anger and great conflict over being Greek and female. And much ambivalence. On the one hand, they did not wish to denigrate their parents, their ethnic group. They were grateful for what parents had done. On the other hand, a look at where a brother is in terms of career achievement and financial independence and where the Greek American woman finds herself in comparison and anger bubbles up. One woman was even angrier than most, because her "brother" was not her father's blood child. He was an adopted orphan, a refugee from the Civil War of Greece. Her financially com-

[7]Constantina Safilios-Rothschild, "Honour Crimes in Contemporary Greece." *The British Journal of Sociology*, 2, no. 2 (June 1969), 205-18.

fortable father chose to arrange a marriage for her rather than educate her. Her "brother" has a Ph.D., an education encouraged and sponsored financially by her father.

In the face of such contradiction and blatant favoritism toward male success, how does one survive, how does one prevent madness? One denies. One sublimates and throws herself into more and more activity acceptable to her parents and community, bears many children and buries herself in volunteer work which becomes a way of life, an outlet for talent and creativity, rather than a legitimate use of spare time. A natural bent for leadership and organizational skills which would stand one in good stead in the running of the family business (or going into politics?) becomes used for such acceptable roles as president of the local ladies fundraising auxiliary. We needn't wonder from what sourse emanates the female energy that Greek American women all over the U.S. pour into fundraising for their church, into year-long cooking and baking marathons for annual church festivals. Frustration and anger must be released in some way; and it is wisely nurtured by its beneficiaries, churches all over the United States whose coffers are filled with the profits from these lucrative affairs.

Dealing with the anger, seeking counseling or going back to school to recapture that missed opportunity is seldom considered an option. One wouldn't get much support for that option anyway. One woman told me that she had wanted to tie up this loose end in her life by returning to college. She asked her mother if she wouldn't consent to take care of her pre-school children two nights a week so she could go to school and earn her degree. Her mother refused. This same mother, however, had never before refused to watch the children so that she could bake and do volunteer work for the local Greek church.

Greek American women come from a culture that, colorful as it is to outside tourists (and make no mistake, attendees at Church festivals are just that: tourists), simply has not been kind to its women. Women in Greece just got the right to vote in 1953. As late as the early '80s, 74 percent of illiterate citizens of Greece were women. Legal consideration of a woman as parent to her child is a relatively recent phenomenon in the mother country.[8] Dowries, contrary to misconceptions of Greeks in America, legally reverted to husbands after marriage. They were not the property of their owners, supposedly the females who brought them into the marriage. Divorce was unheard of, largely because women were not awarded custody of their children. What woman would consider leaving even an abusive marriage without her children, unless she freely chose to do so, and was awarded visitation rights, a concept eliciting derision from any Greek man-on-the-street?

Our mother culture does everything in its power to embolden and empower young boys and men and everything in its power to dominate, control and disenfranchise women. We here in America have done no better in the name of "Tradition with a Capital T," as Eva Topping called it.[9] We are told we must submit to Tradition when we rebel against the words "submit and obey" in the marriage ceremony. We are told we must submit to Tradition when we protest that we may desire to postpone marriage and the bearing of children until completion of our education, no matter how long it may take. Tradition, we are told, dictates that young women shall not have sexual freedom and be allowed to date. We do just about everything we can do to assure that females are under control, their behavior predictable and constricted. We confine any power women might be allowed to possess to the domestic sphere, where they can be guaranteed to do little harm.[10]

Women in contemporary Greece have outpaced Greek Americans. In the last ten years or so, we have witnessed an explosion in Greece of public female power, but decidedly not the traditionally touted variety of illusory and questionable power which makes a woman "queen of the home." This type of "power" is often posed by its apologists as an example of "matriarchy" in our mother country. It is exceedingly difficult to conceive of the power a woman possesses if she is illiterate

[8]Lili Bita, "No Masters But Ourselves." *The Miami Herald*. February 10, 1983.

[9]Eva Catafygiotu Topping, "Orthodox Eve and Her Church." Paper presented at a meeting of The Women's Board of the Patriarch Athenagoras Institute, November 1988.

[10]It is here, however, where the frustrated woman can do the most harm, and much of it unwittingly, for she takes out her rage on the most helpless of all of us, infants and young children. This is power?

and cannot vote, much less leave her "kingdom," the family home, except at certain hours, without some type of accompaniment, even for such seemingly routine tasks as shopping for shoes or underwear.

How, then, can this "powerful" citizen of her nation affect whether or not her country goes to war, and her sons are maimed and killed, or defend her daughter from rape, or herself from violent abuse? How, then, is she able to participate in the course of her planet's future, much less that of her nation, or, closer to home, that of her family? Such a woman has little power which outlives her usefulness as *mana* (mother).

Of course, as did Medea, she can slaughter her sons in the privacy of her "kingdom," thereby in some twisted, revengeful way exert her final claim to such "power." Or, presumably, she can deny food to her infant children. Clytemnaestra, it should be recalled, was "queen" of *her* kingdom, the home. However, at the end of the tragedy, she possessed absolutely no power (persuasive or otherwise) which prevented the blood sacrifice of her child to her husband's male pride.

Power is both a primal word and a primal relationship under patriarchy. Through control of the mother, the man assures himself of possession of his children; through control of his children he insures the disposition of his patrimony and the safe passage of his soul after death.[11]

For, as much as she may act as the coequal provider or so-called matriarch within her own family, every mother must deliver her children over within a few years of their birth to the patriarchal system of education, of law, of religion, of sexual codes; she is, in fact, *expected* to prepare them to enter that system without rebelliousness or "maladjustment" and to perpetuate it in their own adult lives.[12]

---

[11]Adrienne Rich, *Of Women Born: Motherhood as Experience and Institution.* (New York: W. W. Norton & Co., 1976), p. 36.
[12]Ibid., p. 39.

Change has come to the mother country. Life for women in Greece today is not the same as it was and the old ways will not return.[18] Women's faces are in the news, women's voices speak from positions of political power, women's names identify national leaders. I see the names of organizations for Greek women and feminist support groups devoted to issues of concern to women, founded by and for women. And I am proud. Proud to be related to these Greek women, to take them as a role model for my own life.

A corresponding enthusiasm for liberation has not evidenced itself among Greek American women. Where are the female counterparts in the second generation of Greek Americans to Sarbanes, to Dukakis, and to Petris? Where is a presence in academia, in the business world, in finance, in law, in medicine, that corresponds to the incredible numbers of our men? In my recent interviews, I find to my increasing disappointment and chagrin that twenty years of the women's movement seems to have failed to inspire young women of Greek descent. Young Greek American women in large numbers still persist in marrying the career rather than having it for themselves, drawing self-esteem and community approval from being identified as appendage to their husbands, in the role as "wife," rather than as achiever in their own right. Those who do pursue careers report that they are presented with incredible pressure around age 30 to give it up and "settle down and be a real Greek woman in a Greek home, with a husband and a family."

What does that mean? What is a "Real Greek Woman?" What is a "Real Greek Home?" And why are our young men not being exhorted to marry and form "Real Greek Homes?" The sad fact is that for us here in America, the "Real Greek Home" and the "Real Greek Family" is woman's domain. If there is to be genuine Greek culture and ethnicity in this country the burden of its maintenance is placed on women. Therein lies the same dilemma for the young third- and fourth-generation Greek American woman as existed sixty or seventy years ago

[18]Maria Maghiorou, "History of the Greek Women's Movement," in: *Foreign Women in Greece*. Athens, Greece: Eleftheros Typos, 1984. See also: doctoral thesis by Maghiorou, "Mouvement Social et Politique des Femmes en Grece, 1875-1980." Universite de Paris X - Nanterre, Ecole des Hautes Etudes en Sciences Sociales, 1982.

for *Yaya*. During her early years here (according to my interviews with first-generation Greek immigrant women), *Yaya*
struggled with the problem of family loyalty versus self-realiza-
tion in the most limited way. She had to decide whether to go
to the American school and learn English and thus participate
in the outside world or to behave as a Greek woman and stay
in the community. These first-wave women by and large decided
(not necessarily on their own, but with "friendly persuasion" of
their fathers-husbands) to cut themselves off from the *xeni*.
Yaya decided to stay home, raise her family, and build her
church. Exclusively.

Is that a viable and even desirable goal for young women
of the '80s and '90s, twenty years after the current wave of
feminism? There can be no doubt that young Greek American
women are every bit as creative and brilliant as Greek American
men, albeit in some ways crippled by their conflict. It is in
their twenties that they most need encouragement and a healthy
dose of cheerleading and affirmation from their community and
from their mothers and fathers to complete their educations.
This is, however, the time of their lives when the opposite occurs, when they receive negative feedback, and are subtly and
not-so-subtly guided into abandonment of worthy educational
goals that require dedication, long hours of study, and isolation
from "social life" or the pursuit of marriage.

Is it fair of parents to require of a female child a sacrifice not
required of her brother? What parent would discourage a
young Greek American male from completion of his medical
degree because he had not yet married? Who has ever heard
of a promising Greek American male career in law or philosophy
stopped dead in its tracks by the "necessity" for marriage and
family NOW? Not one of the younger women between the
ages of 22 and 35 responded that she would not ever get married or have a family. She merely desired that the timing of that
event would be her choice, and that the subject would cease to
be the primary topic of discussion with her extended family,
who devalued her education.

I asked these young women what they think our culture
does to encourage leadership among its women. In some cases
the question elicited immediate laughter, as if I should already

know the answer. I did. But I wanted to hear what they had to say about the question. "Good Greek Girls are taught to cook, to sew, to take care of the house and be good churchwomen." This response from a 32-year-old woman born of second-generation American-born parents. She is Greek Orthodox by choice, but does not consider herself a Good Greek Girl. She bought herself a house at 26, owns her own business, and is a financial analyst for a major corporation in Los Angeles. But she chooses not to be a Good Greek Girl, because to be one means doing double and even triple duty. You work hard, but you have to iron your husband's shirts. You have not only to cook, but to cook "Greek," which entails as much effort as being a French chef. You shouldn't embarrass your husband in public by speaking when he is expounding on a subject, not even if you happen to know more about the subject he is talking about than he does. It's not "Greek" to do that. They describe to me a world that I thought was gone.

Another of the questions I asked the women I interviewed was: what is the meaning of the word "freedom" to you? Overwhelmingly, the response I heard most often was, "Freedom to marry whomever I choose. No arranged marriage for me." I still hear the response from women in their 20s and 30s. That this question continues to be an issue tells me something that these women have observed and feel is a very real part of our community. The phrase "freedom to choose" doesn't mean the same thing to our women that it might mean to young women outside Greek America, those who have moved beyond the basics of female psychic and physical survival.

For most non-Greek American women of our era "freedom to choose" denotes options about where to live, whether or not to marry, whether or not to bear children, what school to go to or not to go to. For contemporary Greek American women to define the phrase "freedom to choose" as narrowly as they have done so to me in these interviews signifies that we haven't moved at all. If who we marry is more important than what we achieve, it follows then that we are no better off than the first frightened picture brides who timidly stepped off boats and trains with tags on their clothes that told the world who they were and where to send them, because they did not know the language of the new country.[14] Are we to perpetuate ignorance into later generations using much more insidious psychological and emotional punishment, handicapping our girl children before they have left their cradles?

What have we accomplished if we send our daughters to college without the unconditional support and cheerleading that we give to our sons? What have we accomplished if, in 1989, a 28-year-old woman with a Master's Degree in International Politics tells me of the secret rage she has harbored in her heart against her father since she was 17; anger at him for promising to pay for her education at the Sorbonne if she just was a good girl and kept up her grades and listened to him; and then at the moment of her acceptance, tells her that he has changed his mind, she should live at home and forget about the Sorbonne. Go to school here, he says to her.

There is absolutely no disputing the fact that if the young woman had been her father's male child, rather than his female child, he would not have hesitated at the honor bestowed upon himself and his people of one of his children studying International Relations at the Sorbonne. I was thunderstruck when she told me that she was married with a child at 19. She finished her education, but only with the utmost perseverance. "I would not recommend that anybody try to go to school the way I did." Her father paid for her schooling. But to this day, she doesn't know what to do with the anger surrounding her memories of that period of her life. She had not told anybody about it.

A 29-year-old Ph.D. candidate in Astrophysics confided to me that she doesn't know if she can summon up the emotional energy to finish, because she is so tired of her parents nagging at her to get married and stop pursuing an unwomanly (Un-Greek-womanly) kind of life. Her brother, also a Ph.D. Candidate in Math and Physics, has received no such admonitions regarding his education, and no one has suggested to him that there might be a conflict between his degree and his personal life, no matter what he decides to do, marry or not marry, have

[14]Helen Zeese Papanikolas, *Toil and Rage in a New Land: The Greek Immigrants in Salt Lake City, Utah.* (Salt Lake City, Utah: Utah Historical Society Publication, 1974.)

children or not have children. No one has threatened him with
the loss of his identity as a Greek man if he chooses never to
marry or to finish his degree and become a professor. "It's
taken me so long to even convince them of my right to have
this education. It has sapped me. It has drained me of energy
I need for the studying and the research."

A 29-year-old Vice President of Finance at a major financial
institution in Chicago is in tears after one of my lectures there,
relating to me a similar story. Only this time the mother and
father had been quite specific. She had failed as a human being.
No matter what she does, what she achieves, she is a failure as
a Greek woman if she has not married by this time.

A 25-year-old attorney newly admitted to the California Bar
attends a seminar in Los Angeles on the Greek American Woman
and asks the question: is there something about Greek culture
that would prevent a woman from going into politics and the
public sector? The reply is that any woman who wishes to enter
politics must build a power base. I later interview this woman,
who tells me that she sees very little chance for the Greek American woman with political ambitions to successfully build political power bases among Greek Americans. Citing her perception
of Greek women in America as jealous, gossipy, and in general
the most unsupportive of other women's efforts she knows, she
expresses doubt that Greek American women's organizations
would be willing to work very hard to garner support for another Greek American woman's rise to power. She would go
first to Greek American men. Even then she would be wary.

The Greek American woman of the '80s faces serious questions about "being Greek." She desires to affirm Greek female
identity in some way that would not force her to compromise
freedom and choices. One of her choices, in increasingly large
numbers, is to leave the community for a different and, what
she perceives to be, a better life. She outmarries more often
than her male counterpart.

Growing up, she has had few role models. Those that could
have been role models, the first pathfinders who became lawyers,
professors, and businesswomen usually outmarried or left, never
to be heard from again. One of these accomplished women, a
judge, tells me that as an educated woman, she remembers

being talked about at her local Greek church. Not having much interest in the traditional preoccupations of the women of the church in fundraising and teaching Sunday School, she was viewed as an "uppity" woman who thought she was better than other women.

Unfortunately, we have an insidious method of discouraging our own betterment through self-hatred passed out among ourselves in generous doses. Greek American women are masters at the putdown, the innuendo, the gossipy exclusion of the educated woman, the woman of accomplishment.

We learned these lessons in mind and behavior control of each other from our grandmothers and mothers, at the same time we were learning techniques in the best way to bake a pan of *tiropita* or *spanakopita*. We were taught by example about assassination of each other in the basement kitchens of the church, behavior encouraged by a church hierarchy that refuses recognition of any female achievement outside the bounds of production of male children.

Possibly it is an advantage, this tacit compliance in the perpetuation of our roles as Thought Police of each other. Thus it is that the men escape responsibility for overt negativity. They are not called to answer for ignoring woman as human being and equal, for rendering her invisible as Sacred Being, because woman herself has been socialized to control her own and other women's behavior, to keep silence, following rules that are not her own creation. Even our history in the Church has been buried, our myriad women saints and religious heroines ignored in favor of the one all-holy passive Panayia, our only female role model for spirituality, the Virgin Mother.[15]

Change is threatening. Change is painful. But change will come, if we are truly interested in the best and brightest of our daughters, and wish for them equal participation in their community, in the world beyond their community, and for the expansion of their roles and choices, their growth as human beings. Not only the blatantly obvious omissions must be attended to, but the myriad daily discounting of the female's contributions and the routine hobbling of her mind and psyche,

[15]Eva Catafygiotu Topping, *Holy Mothers of Orthodoxy*. (Minneapolis, Minnesota: Light and Life Publishing, 1987.)

the thousand little ways in which we wound her, must cease
to be a part of Tradition, must cease to be a part of our definition
of ethnicity in the United States.

Contributors

THE EDITORS:

DAN GEORGAKAS teaches at the Van Arsdale School of Labor Studies, Empire State College, State University of New York. He has written extensively on ethnicity in America, film, and labor. Among other works, he has written the introduction to and coedited *Solidarity Forever: An Oral History of the IWW*, coauthored *Detroit: I Do Mind Dying*, and coedited *The Encyclopedia of the American Left*.

CHARLES C. MOSKOS is professor of sociology at Northwestern University. He has been a fellow at the Woodrow Wilson International Center for Scholars and a Rockefeller Humanities Fellow. His books include *A Call to Civic Service, The Military—More Than Just a Job?* and *Greek Americans: Struggle and Success*. His writings have been translated into seven languages.

THE AUTHORS:

CONSTANCE CALLINICOS, a longtime feminist and activist for women's rights, has most recently concentrated her activism and writing on the subject of becoming female among Greeks in America and in the mother country, Greece. She has published articles and lectured widely on a variety of topics germane to this subject (including an exploration of arranged marriages and the dowry system as it exists in Greek America). In her work, she wishes not only to document this world for those who were born into it (and at the same time raise consciousness), but also to illuminate its complexities for those unfamiliar with it.

HELEN GERACIMOS CHAPIN was born in Hawaii of parents from Sparta. She is professor of English and vice president and dean for the satellite programs at Hawaii Pacific College, Honolulu. She is editor of *Hawaiian Journal of History*.

PETER W. DICKSON (DIKAIOS) has served as a political-military analyst at the Central Intelligence Agency since 1971. He is an author of an intellectual biography of Henry Kissinger. He is third-generation Tsintzinian through his father's family.

181

YIORGOS KALOGERAS is assistant professor of American ethnic and minority literature, English department, Aristotle University, Thessaloniki, Greece. He has published essays on ethnic literature in Greek and English in journals in the United States and Greece.

ALEXANDROS K. KYROU is a doctoral candidate in modern Greek and East European history at Indiana University, where he received his B.A. and M.A. degrees in history. He is a member of several academic associations and is a consultant to the still developing Hellenic Museum and Cultural Center of Chicago.

G. JAMES PATTERSON, professor of anthropology at Eastern Oregon State College, has been studying Greek immigrants in the West for some twenty years. His two books on the subject are *The Greeks of Vancouver: A Study in the Preservation of Ethnicity* and *The Unassimilated Greeks of Denver*.

GUNTHER W. PECK is a doctoral candidate in American history at the University of Wisconsin—Madison. His work on Skliris and Greek laborers is part of a larger study comparing the relationship between ethnicity and labor radicalism in two Western company towns: Lead, South Dakota, and Bingham, Utah. He was a recipient of the Jacob Javits Fellowship (U.S. Department of Education), 1988-1989.

OLE L. SMITH teaches modern Greek history and social sciences in the department of modern Greek and Balkan studies, University of Copenhagen, Denmark. He has written extensively on the history of the Greek Communist Party and Greek worker movements. He is currently doing research on early rebetika in Greece and the United States.

EVA CATAFYGIOTU TOPPING is best known for her work regarding women in the Orthodox tradition. Her most recent book is *Holy Mothers of Orthodoxy: Women and the Church*. She has been a Fulbright Scholar and has taught Greek and Latin at Wheaton College and the University of Cincinnati.